S. Hrg. 115–47

EMERGENCY MANAGEMENT IN INDIAN COUNTRY: IMPROVING FEMA'S FEDERAL-TRIBAL RELATIONSHIP WITH INDIAN TRIBES

HEARING

BEFORE THE

COMMITTEE ON INDIAN AFFAIRS
UNITED STATES SENATE

ONE HUNDRED FIFTEENTH CONGRESS

FIRST SESSION

FEBRUARY 8, 2017

Printed for the use of the Committee on Indian Affairs

U.S. GOVERNMENT PUBLISHING OFFICE

26–164 PDF　　　　　WASHINGTON : 2017

CONTENTS

EMERGENCY MANAGEMENT IN INDIAN COUNTRY: IMPROVING FEMA'S FEDERAL–TRIBAL RELATIONSHIP WITH INDIAN TRIBES

WEDNESDAY, FEBRUARY 8, 2017

U.S. SENATE,
COMMITTEE ON INDIAN AFFAIRS,
Washington, DC.

The Committee met, pursuant to notice, at 2:57 p.m. in room 628, Dirksen Senate Office Building, Hon. John Hoeven, Chairman of the Committee, presiding.

OPENING STATEMENT OF HON. JOHN HOEVEN, U.S. SENATOR FROM NORTH DAKOTA

The CHAIRMAN. We will now commence the oversight hearing on Emergency Management in Indian Country: Improving FEMA's Federal-Tribal Relationship with Indian Tribes.

The Committee is holding this important hearing on emergency management in Indian country. It is timely to begin this conversation now.

The winters can be hazardous in many parts of the country. With the spring comes the thaw and often flooding. My home State of North Dakota is a good example. In other parts of the country, oftentimes it is tornadoes or battling fires.

Some Indian reservations in North Dakota, most notably the Spirit Lake Indian Reservation and the Turtle Mountain Band of Chippewa, have received major disaster declarations due to spring flooding.

Tribes around the country experience other types of emergencies and disasters. These hard hit communities face a long road to recovery. It is incumbent upon the Federal Emergency Management Agency, FEMA, to effectively assist in that recovery and to get an early start on efforts to reduce the impacts of future disaster risks. Tribes can seek emergency aid for emergency declarations directly from the President, instead of going through the States. This is designed to help with timely requests and timely assistance to hard hit communities.

Today, we will hear from the witnesses regarding these events and the Federal response, as well as recommendations for improving emergency management and the Federal-tribal relationship.

Before we turn to our witnesses, I want to ask Vice Chairman Udall if he has an opening statement?

STATEMENT OF HON. TOM UDALL,
U.S. SENATOR FROM NEW MEXICO

Senator UDALL. Yes, I do, Mr. Chairman.

Thank you for calling this oversight hearing so quickly into the new Congress. Tribal disaster declaration authority is critical to tribal governments across the country.

I look forward to working with you on this issue and others that require deliberate and focused congressional oversight.

Before I begin my opening remarks, I would like to welcome and thank the tribal witnesses, two of whom represent tribes from my home State of New Mexico. Both Governor Chavarria of the Santa Clara Pueblo and President Begaye of the Navajo Nation have shown strong leadership and dedication to tribal self determination and self governance, particularly in managing natural disasters on their tribal homelands.

In 2015, 3 million gallons of toxic mine water swept downstream into the Navajo Nation's lands following the rupture of the Gold King Mine in Colorado. As President Begaye can attest, we still do not know the full impacts of this environmental disaster that sent polluted water into the Animas and San Juan Rivers and through the Navajo Nation.

The Federal Government response to Gold King has been one of the most frustrating things I have seen the Navajo Nation go through in my time in Congress. In response, working with a bipartisan group of colleagues, we enacted the legislation last year to prioritize government reimbursements and to fund and authorize long term water quality monitoring.

Now the Federal Government is denying liability for personal damage claims, including for Navajo farmers. This is unacceptable to me. We are now again working on new legislation to compensate individuals who lost crops and suffered other damages from the spills.

In Santa Clara Pueblo, the Las Conchas fire, one of the largest in New Mexico history, destroyed thousands of acres of Pueblo's traditional lands. Subsequent severe flooding destroyed thousands more. The damage was extensive and devastating to the tribe's canyon and scorched the tribe's watershed.

I have seen the aftermath of this disaster firsthand and I know the watershed restoration project is a major challenge.

As a result of this catastrophic wildfire, the Pueblo has been forced to make five disaster declarations seeking assistance from the Federal Government since 2011. I am proud to say that I supported both the Santa Clara Pueblo and Navajo Nations' emergency declaration requests and letters to the President.

I look forward to hearing about their experience with disaster relief and its impacts. I also look forward to hearing the FEMA witnesses describe the recently issued Tribal Pilot Guidance and the agency's plans for further implementation of the Act.

Since the enactment of the Tribal Stafford Act in 2013, tribes have been able to request emergency or major disaster declarations directly from the President and independent of States. For many years, tribes were forced to rely on their State governor to make these requests on their behalf in order to receive Stafford Act assistance, assistance that is vital to tribal governments for protecting the health and safety of their citizens in the wake of emergency or major disasters.

I strongly support the parity created by the Tribal Stafford Act for tribal and State governments and their concurrent ability to seek disaster assistance directly from the President.

I understand that there are tribal State coordination issues that could result in inadequate Federal assistance for both sovereigns. I look forward to hearing from FEMA and the tribal witnesses today about what actions have been taken to ensure that tribes and States coordinate closely on decisions to request emergency or disaster declarations.

Federal assistance that supports tribal efforts to respond to and recover from an incident that overwhelms tribal capabilities must be effective. That is why I signed onto a Government Accountability Office request to study tribal disaster declaration issues.

This request includes ways to build and strengthen tribal capacity to request major disaster declarations and manage associated funding. I expect the result of this study to inform further bipartisan discussions among my Committee colleagues on how we can work together to assist tribal governments in protecting public health, safety and property in the event of a major disaster in Indian country.

Thank you again, Mr. Chairman.

The CHAIRMAN. Thank you, Vice Chairman Udall.

Are there other opening statements before we turn to the witnesses? Senator Cantwell.

STATEMENT OF HON. MARIA CANTWELL, U.S. SENATOR FROM WASHINGTON

Senator CANTWELL. Mr. Chairman, I would just like to welcome my constituent and witness, Mr. Cody Desautel from the Colville Tribe who is with us here today and thank him for coming.

The Colville Tribe, along with Washington State, has been front and center in two years of devastating fires in 2014 and 2015. We lost 863,000 acres during that time period. In 2015, the Tunk Block and North Star fires devastated the Confederated Tribe of the Colville Reservation and they lost 259,000 acres of commercial timberland which held a billion board feet of salable lumber resulting in a 20 percent loss of their general operating revenues.

If there is any tribe in America that can tell you the devastating impacts of these natural disasters and fires, it is the Colville Reservation.

Thank you, Mr. Desautel, for being with us and being a witness at today's hearing.

The CHAIRMAN. Senator Tester.

STATEMENT OF HON. JON TESTER, U.S. SENATOR FROM MONTANA

Senator TESTER. Very quickly, thank you, Mr. Chairman.

The Black Feet Tribe just declared a state of emergency because they received five feet of snow last night. To rub salt in the wound, they are predicting 50 mile an hour winds tomorrow. They will get help from the State.

I only bring this up because of the timeliness of this hearing. They are going to be calling and will be needing help. You know what happens with 5 feet of snow and 50 mile an hour winds. You also know what happens when it gets above 32 degrees and you have that kind of snow melt.

Thank you all for being here. I especially want to thank the tribes.

The CHAIRMAN. Do other Senators have opening comments? Senator Murkowski.

STATEMENT OF HON. LISA MURKOWSKI,
U.S. SENATOR FROM ALASKA

Senator MURKOWSKI. You gave me an opening. I said we need to get to the witnesses.

Mr. Chairman, I too want to thank you for the timeliness of this hearing. Alaska is pretty legendary for the disasters we have whether they are earthquakes, floods, fires, mudslides or volcanoes. We kind of do it all.

One of the things I am hoping to have discussion about today, I really appreciate the witnesses, is what we are calling a slow moving disaster. That is a reality we are facing in Alaska as we are seeing communities threatened by storms, flooding, coastal erosion, the thaw of our permafrost and the impact to our communities that are considering relocation, asking for assistance with relocation to protect their families and their way of life.

The infrastructure is being severely damaged whether it is the water systems, maybe not water at all, peoples' homes are literally falling into the ocean due to coastal erosion and more are in danger. There are schools and community buildings that are at risk.

Two of the communities that are facing substantial danger right now are the Yupik community of Newtok and Kivalina and the Inupiat community up on the Chukchi. Both of these communities have recently applied for major disaster declarations due to severe storms, flooding and many of the issues I mentioned.

Yet both of these communities were denied because they did not fit the contours of the Stafford Act. It is something that as we are talking about disasters, I think we need to recognize that we have disasters as Senator Tester has just mentioned with the weather that is coming and then we have these disasters that we see coming at us and perhaps not in an immediate forceful way but the force of the looming danger to our communities is very, very real.

I thank you for the opportunity to discuss these important issues today and look forward to the comments from today's witnesses.

The CHAIRMAN. Do other Senators have comments before we turn to the witnesses? Senator Franken.

STATEMENT OF HON. AL FRANKEN,
U.S. SENATOR FROM MINNESOTA

Senator FRANKEN. Thank you, Chairman Hoeven and Vice Chairman Udall for holding this hearing and thank you to all of our witnesses for your testimony.

Before I begin my remarks, I want to take a moment to recognize Senator Barrasso for his leadership as chairman and Senator Tester for his as well in the last Congress.

To our new Chair and new Vice Chairman, I look forward to continuing to work with you in this new Congress.

This hearing is an opportunity to shine a light on the very important relationship between FEMA and the tribes. I will touch on this a bit more in my questions but I am particularly interested to hear about FEMA's relationship with the Prairie Island Indian community.

Prairie Island sits on a floodplain in the Mississippi River. It is also approximately 600 yards from two nuclear reactors and nuclear waste storage facilities. The members of the Prairie Island community live with a constant concern of radiation exposure.

In my State, it is very important that FEMA is prepared for anything and that it continues to coordinate its emergency management plans with Prairie Island.

Thank you again, Mr. Chairman and Vice Chairman Udall. To all the witnesses, I look forward to your testimony.

The CHAIRMAN. Do any other Senators wish comment before we proceed to the witnesses?

Our witnesses today are: Mr. Alex Amparo, Assistant Administrator for Recovery, Office of Response and Recovery, Federal Emergency Management Agency, U.S. Department of Homeland Security; Mr. Milo Booth, National Tribal Affairs Advisor, Office of External Affairs, Federal Emergency Management Agency, U.S. Department of Homeland Security; the Honorable Russell Begaye, President, Navajo Nation, Window Rock, Arizona; the Honorable J. Michael Chavarria, Governor, Pueblo of Santa Clara, Española, New Mexico; and Mr. Cody Desautel, Natural Resources Director, Confederated Tribes of the Colville Reservation, Nespelem, Washington.

I want to remind the witnesses that your full written testimony will be made a part of the official hearing record. If you would, please keep your opening statements to five minutes each so that we proceed to questions.

With that, we will begin with Mr. Amparo.

STATEMENT OF ALEX AMPARO, ASSISTANT ADMINISTRATOR FOR RECOVERY, OFFICE OF RESPONSE AND RECOVERY, FEDERAL EMERGENCY MANAGEMENT AGENCY, U.S. DEPARTMENT OF HOMELAND SECURITY; ACCOMPANIED BY: MILO BOOTH, NATIONAL TRIBAL AFFAIRS ADVISOR, OFFICE OF EXTERNAL AFFAIRS

Mr. AMPARO. Good afternoon and thank you, Chairman Hoeven, Vice Chairman Udall, and members of the Committee.

It is my pleasure to be here today with our National Tribal Advisor, Mr. Milo Booth. Thank you for the opportunity to provide you an update on FEMA's efforts since we last testified in the summer of 2014. I am excited to talk with you about how we have progressed.

FEMA has a long history of working within our authority to fully embrace the nation-to-nation relationship between the U.S. Government and federally recognized tribes. Prior to 2013, as mentioned, tribes had to seek disaster assistance through State declarations.

Thanks to the authority provided to us by Congress with the passage of the Sandy Recovery Improvement Act, tribes now have the option to request a declaration from the President directly.

At FEMA, we applaud this change which properly reflects tribal sovereignty and we work very hard to further our agency's relationship with tribes. I am pleased to share with you that FEMA has released the Tribal Declarations Pilot Guidance which provides new specifically designed criteria for evaluating a tribe's request for a declaration and takes into account the unique effects of tribal nations and conditions.

This guidance was shaped by extensive outreach and communication with our tribal partners. This included three rounds of tribal consultation comprised of 140 listening sessions nationwide. Each round of consultation averaged 500 participants representing approximately one-third of all federally-recognized tribes.

By the end, we had received more than 2,000 comments which we, as an agency carefully reviewed and responded to on our website. Most importantly, this input was vital in shaping the pilot guidance that has been released.

In addition to the development of the declaration guidance, FEMA has undertaken many actions to build and improve relationships with our tribal partners. We have hired a national tribal advisor and a tribal specialist at our headquarters to help lead this activity.

We ensured that each of our ten regions has at least one tribal liaison to work in building that relationship in the field with tribes individually on a regular basis. They help coordinate a variety of services that FEMA can provide to tribes including technical assistance, grant opportunities, exercise training and others. When disaster strikes, we also deploy from our cadre of tribal specialists who are on call.

I tell you from my more than 20 years experience in emergency management that effective emergency management at its core is based on relationships, understanding mutual capacities and the needs of communities. From this foundation, we then enhance disaster preparedness through targeted planning, training and exercises.

FEMA's Emergency Management Institute and the Center for Domestic Preparedness, two of our main training facilities, have developed tribal-specific training. For example, in 2016, more than 1,000 tribal emergency managers and first responders were trained in these facilities.

In fact, in just a few weeks at the Center for Domestic Preparedness, we will host the second annual tribal nations training week which includes multiple courses for training first responders, followed by a full scale integrated exercise. Last year, over 157 tribal emergency managers and 46 tribal nations participated.

Outside of our training facilities, FEMA is also facilitating more large scale exercises to support building tribal response capabilities. Last year, FEMA Region 10 in the Northwest conducted the Cascadia Rising, a four day earthquake and tsunami exercise. Twenty-four tribes in Washington, Oregon and Idaho participated in various ways ranging from tsunami evacuation drills to full integration in local emergency operations centers.

What I have outlined today illustrates just a part of our commitment to federally-recognized tribal governments.

Thank you for the opportunity to talk to you about the work the men and women at FEMA have done. FEMA continues to be committed to our partnership and collaboration with tribes.

There is still much work for us to do. We recognize that and remain committed to Indian country and working with this Committee and our tribal partners to learn, evolve and help build a more resilient America.

Thank you for your time and I look forward to the questions of this Committee.

[The prepared statement of Mr. Amparo follows:]

PREPARED STATEMENT OF ALEX AMPARO, ASSISTANT ADMINISTRATOR FOR RECOVERY, OFFICE OF RESPONSE AND RECOVERY, FEDERAL EMERGENCY MANAGEMENT AGENCY, U.S. DEPARTMENT OF HOMELAND SECURITY

Introduction

Good afternoon, Chairman Hoeven, Vice Chairman Udall, and members of the Committee. I am Alex Amparo, Assistant Administrator with the U.S. Department of Homeland Security's (DHS) Federal Emergency Management Agency (FEMA). Thank you for this opportunity to meet with you today to discuss ways in which FEMA is improving relationships with federally recognized Indian tribes.

FEMA is committed to our partnership and collaboration with federally recognized Indian tribes, and to providing support in their preparation for, protection against, mitigation of, response to, and recovery from all hazards and disasters. FEMA has a strong tradition of engagement with federally recognized Indian tribal governments (tribal governments). However, since the passage of the Sandy Recovery Improvement Act (SRIA) in 2013, the agency has dedicated additional resources to ensuring that tribal governments are fully woven into the fabric of our mission. Today, I can tell you that FEMA recognizes the unique relationship between In- dian Country and the Federal Government, and the unique conditions that affect Indian Country. We work side-by-side with our tribal partners on all aspects of our mission, and we continue to posture ourselves to better support our tribal partners at any time. To reinforce how we recognize these important relationships, I would like to specifically outline FEMA's approach as described in: (1) FEMA's Tribal Pol- icy; (2) FEMA's Tribal Consultation Policy; and, (3) FEMA's Tribal Declaration Pilot Guidance.

FEMA's Tribal Policy

The U.S. Government has a unique nation-to-nation relationship with federally recognized tribal governments based on the Constitution of the United States, treaties, statutes, executive orders, and judicial decisions. In 2016, FEMA updated its agency-wide tribal policy. The policy outlines a framework for nation-to-nation relations with federally recognized tribal governments that recognizes tribal sovereignty, self-governance, and the general trust relationship, consistent with applicable authorities.

Key principles of our policy include:

A. Recognizing the unique nature of each tribal community and the need to work with all members of tribal communities, FEMA commits to building strong and lasting partnerships with tribal governments to assist in preparing for all threats and hazards, including those unique to tribal communities.

B. FEMA will respect and support the unique status of sovereign tribal governments by engaging in meaningful dialogue that will assist tribal communities with any emergency management needs, which fall under the authority of FEMA.

C. FEMA acknowledges the inherent sovereignty of tribal governments, the general trust relationship with the federal government, and the nation-to-nation relationship between the U.S. Government and tribal governments as established by the U.S. Constitution, statutes, treaties, court decisions, executive orders, regulations, and policies as the foundation of this policy.

In updating this policy, FEMA conducted tribal consultation in 2016, to facilitate tribal feedback on the proposed policy revisions. FEMA held 23 separate events nationwide consisting of 18 regional in-person listening sessions, two national webinars, and three tribal association conference presentations during the tribal consultation period reaching more than 300 tribal participants. FEMA received more than 100 comments in-person and through email, which the agency adjudicated to finalize this revised policy.

For FEMA, this consultation effort on the updated FEMA Tribal Policy represented a significant outreach. To accomplish this FEMA developed structures throughout the agency to support improving our relationships with federally recognized Indian tribal governments. In 2014, FEMA hired a National Tribal Affairs Advisor, Milo Booth (Tsimpshian from the Metlakatla Indian Community in Metlakatla, Alaska), to lead the Tribal Partners Branch (TPB) at FEMA headquarters. In 2016, Margeau Valteau (Navajo from Window Rock, Arizona) joined the TPB as a tribal specialist.

FEMA tribal liaisons, located in our regional offices, are the first resource and point of contact for tribal nations that have questions or require technical assistance on agency programs. Following the federal recognition of the Pamunkey Indian Tribe in 2016, FEMA added a Regional Tribal Liaison to FEMA Region III giving each FEMA regional office at least one tribal liaison supporting tribal affairs. While these tribal liaisons are a critical piece to our outreach and work with tribal governments, it is important to know that all FEMA employees who administer our various programs are available to assist in delivering programs and resources to Indian Country.

In addition to Tribal Affairs staffing, FEMA's Emergency Management Institute (EMI) provides training to tribal governments and their employees to develop their emergency management capabilities. During fiscal year 2016, EMI delivered 55 tribal courses to 763 tribal attendees and 94 other partners. The tribal curriculum courses are delivered by a team of instructors who are selected for their extensive experience working with and for tribal governments in emergency management and the majority of the instructors are tribal members. In addition to providing tribal curriculum courses on the EMI campus in Emmitsburg, Maryland, EMI also provides these courses off-site, traveling out to Indian Country to reach tribal communities directly. EMI currently has planned 21 courses on their 2017 schedule, and will likely increase course deliveries as the year progresses.

FEMA's Center for Domestic Preparedness (CDP) provides training to tribal emergency responders. In fiscal year 2016, CDP hosted its first Tribal Training Week and trained 157 tribal emergency responders from 46 tribal nations. During the week, CDP conducted five courses followed by an operational Integrated Capstone Event full-scale exercise. In 2016, 793 tribal first responders completed courses at the CDP, a 245 percent increase from 2015. This year CDP will host the 2017 Tribal Nations Training Week from March 19 to 25.

Exercises

In addition to providing training, FEMA also coordinates exercises with tribal nations to examine and validate capabilities critical to their readiness.

In September 2015, in Great Falls, Montana, more than 100 people came together to simulate the response to crude oil train derailment on the Blackfeet Nation. FEMA's National Exercise Division coordinated the exercise, Montana Operation Safe Delivery, along with Blackfeet Nation, the State of Montana, and FEMA Region VIII staff. This is one of three in a nationwide series of exercises and the only one to take place on a tribal nation. The goal of the exercise was to examine and confirm the capabilities needed to respond to, reduce the effects of, mitigate the consequences of, and recover from a train derailment involving crude oil. The two-day seminar and tabletop exercise brought together all seven tribal nations in Montana to participate in and learn from a simulated volatile incident.

In June 2016, FEMA Region X conducted a four-day functional earthquake and tsunami exercise, Cascadia Rising. At least 24 tribes in Washington, Oregon, and Idaho participated in various ways ranging from tsunami evacuation drills to full integration in the local Emergency Operations Center. During Cascadia Rising, FEMA exercised its internal capacity to respond to multiple direct disaster declarations from tribal governments.

Tribal participation continues to improve our discussions about pre-landfall hurricane preparedness as well. For the third year in 2016, tribal emergency managers participated in FEMA's annual hurricane preparedness video teleconference with FEMA leadership and state emergency management directors in hurricane-prone areas.

By both providing staff resources at the national and regional level, as well as mission critical training opportunities for tribes, FEMA gains a better understanding of the unique circumstances that affect tribal governments and identifies creative solutions to these unique challenges to better partner with tribal governments and emergency management professionals to serve the needs of disaster survivors.

FEMA Tribal Consultation Policy

FEMA's Tribal Consultation Policy governs precisely how we engage Indian tribes in meaningful consultation. It was developed and issued pursuant to E.O. 13175 of November 6, 2000, *Consultation and Coordination with Indian Tribal Governments* and Presidential Memorandum, *Tribal Consultation* (74 Fed. Reg. 57881) that direct agencies to engage in regular and meaningful consultation and collaboration with tribal officials in the development of federal policies that have tribal implications, and to strengthen the government-to-government relationship between the United States and Indian tribes.

The current consultation policy was signed in August 2014, and outlines the specific roles and responsibilities for various FEMA officials, as well as a detailed outline on how consultation is achieved and when it takes place. As a result of this policy, if a tribal government was not consulted on an existing policy or action by FEMA that they determine affects their community or has tribal implications, they may contact the National Tribal Affairs Advisor and request to be a consulting party. Much like how the FEMA Tribal Policy was updated, we anticipate updating the FEMA Tribal Consultation Policy in 2017. We look forward to engaging our tribal partners during the comment period to ensure that our update reflects the evolving needs of Indian Country.

Underlying FEMA's work and mission is the whole community approach that reinforces that FEMA is only one part of our nation's emergency management team. We must leverage all of our collective team resources in preparing for, protecting against, responding to, recovering from, and mitigating against all hazards. Tribal nations are critical components in our whole community, and our commitment to addressing their needs is evident in our strategic priority to be survivor-centric in mission and program delivery. To further survivor-centric outcomes, FEMA leadership adopted a "cut the red tape" posture to focus on the needs of survivors and to develop and execute programs and policies with survivors' perspectives in mind. FEMA recognizes that the consistent participation and partnership of tribal governments is vital in helping FEMA achieve its mission, so an ongoing dialogue with tribal governments and periodic updates of our policies is key to ensuring these goals are met.

FEMA's Tribal Declaration Pilot Guidance

On January 29, 2013, President Obama signed into law the Sandy Recovery Improvement Act of 2013 (P.L. 113–2) (SRIA), one of the most significant pieces of legislation impacting disaster response and recovery since the Post-Katrina Emergency Management Reform Act of 2006.

Section 1110 of SRIA, "Tribal Requests for a Major Disaster or Emergency Declaration under the Stafford Act" authorized federally recognized Indian tribal governments (tribal governments) the option to request a Stafford Act emergency or major disaster declaration independent of the state if they chose to do so. As amended, the Stafford Act now better reflects the sovereignty of tribal governments and acknowledges FEMA's nation-to-nation relationship with tribal governments. This new authority also requires the President to "consider the unique conditions that affect the general welfare of Indian tribal governments" when issuing regulations to implement this new authority. FEMA developed a phased implementation to ensure consideration of the unique needs of tribal governments, which are further outlined below.

In consultation with federally recognized tribal governments, we are working thoughtfully and deliberately to develop regulations that best reflect the unique situation of tribal governments. Therefore, FEMA began implementing the new authority in three phases: (1) use of adapted state regulations; (2) implementation of pilot guidance; and (3) final rulemaking.

Immediate Use of Regulations

Immediately after SRIA's enactment, FEMA used existing state declaration regulations and criteria to process declaration requests from tribal governments. Since the passage of SRIA, there have been eight major disasters declared in Indian Country: The Eastern Band of Cherokee Indians (North Carolina), the Navajo Nation (Arizona, New Mexico, and Utah), the Standing Rock Sioux Tribe (North Dakota and South Dakota), the Karuk Tribe (California), the Santa Clara Pueblo Tribe

(New Mexico), which has received two disaster declarations, the Soboba Band of Luiseno Indians (California), and the Oglala Sioux Tribe of the Pine Ridge Reservations (South Dakota). Through these declarations, Public Assistance, Individual Assistance, and Hazard Mitigation Grant Program funding is being provided directly to the tribal governments.

On February 14, 2013, the Eastern Band of Cherokee Indians (EBCI) submitted a request for a declaration due to severe weather which resulted in flooding, road damage, and landslides in the EBCI Qualla Boundary and associated lands. A Major Disaster Declaration was signed on March 1, 2013, as the first direct federal to tribe disaster declaration under SRIA. The tribe's existing relationship with the state of North Carolina and the FEMA Region IV Tribal Liaison was strengthened and additional connections with FEMA were created during the event. These connections allowed less turmoil for the tribe when performing multiple processes and mission support in an environment of inexperienced applicants. Lessons learned included clarification and guidance regarding policies and procedures on tribal declarations and the need for more cultural awareness by FEMA staff.

In August 2015, the President declared a disaster for the Oglala Sioux tribe as a result of severe storms, straight line winds, and flooding. As part of the assistance made available through the disaster declaration, FEMA and the Oglala Sioux Tribe completed a permanent housing construction mission that delivered 196 manufactured homes, and repaired an additional 107 homes on the tribe's Pine Ridge Indian Reservation. The housing mission was part of the first ever Presidential major disaster declaration for Individual Assistance granted directly to a tribal nation. The agency hired 25 local tribal members to assist in that effort and their roles were vital in the success of the mission. In addition, following the disaster, eleven tribal members joined the FEMA Reservist program.

FEMA gathered critical information, best practices, and process challenges that have informed the development of the *Tribal Declarations Pilot Guidance* that serves as a comprehensive resource for tribal governments on Stafford Act declarations, disaster assistance, and related requirements.

Pilot Guidance Development

FEMA's disaster declaration regulations were developed to evaluate states' capacity and their need for supplemental disaster assistance. Since these parameters may not be indicative of a tribal nation's ability to respond and recover from a disaster, FEMA augmented its procedures and criteria to reflect the capacity and needs of tribal governments. Before entering the rulemaking process, FEMA intends to utilize the pilot period to inform the development of regulations, ultimately leading to final regulations which reflect the unique needs of tribal governments.

Tribal participation and input was critical to the development of the Tribal Declarations Pilot Guidance. In 2013, FEMA initiated tribal consultation to inform the development of the first draft guidance. FEMA hosted 26 listening sessions nationwide. FEMA sent written correspondence from the FEMA Administrator to all 567 federally recognized tribes, and issued advisories to national and regional tribal organizations and associations to advise them of the consultation. FEMA regional and headquarters leadership presented at numerous tribal conferences to provide an overview of the declaration process and to solicit feedback.

In 2014, FEMA conducted 60 listening sessions around the country, from Northern Alaska to Montana, Oklahoma to Florida, and to Maine with 540 participants and 220 tribes represented. Through these listening sessions, FEMA gathered more than 1,000 comments on the first draft guidance as well as strengthened relationships with tribal governments. We learned more about the challenges that tribal communities face, the response and recovery capabilities of tribal governments, and their understanding of Stafford Act assistance. FEMA regions have been extremely proactive in meeting consultation requests of Native Alaskan Villages and Indian tribal governments. For instance, FEMA Region X senior staff flew to Alaska to consult with the Aleut Communities of St. Paul and St. George Islands.

The second draft of the guidance was posted to the Federal Register for a 90-day public comment period that ended in April 2016. In addition to posting in the Federal Register, FEMA conducted additional consultation over the 90-day period with over 500 tribal officials representing 178 federally recognized tribal governments through participation in 54 listening sessions nationwide. Nearly 800 comments were received and adjudicated. The final Tribal Declarations Pilot Guidance is a culmination of all of the interaction and feedback through consultation with tribal governments that has occurred over the past several years. In total, FEMA received over 2,000 comments and conducted 140 listening sessions nationwide.

The pilot guidance describes the process by which tribal governments will use to request Stafford Act declarations, during the pilot period, and the criteria FEMA will use to evaluate direct tribal declaration requests and make a recommendation to the President. It is the culmination of over three years of tribal consultation and development of multiple drafts of the guidance. The guidance incorporates key changes based on comments FEMA received from tribes. These changes include the establishment of a Public Assistance minimum damage amount for tribal declarations of $250,000; the addition of historic preservation as a demographic factor that may influence the impacts of a disaster; expansion of eligibility under the Individuals and Households Program to include non-enrolled tribal community members, when requested by the tribal government; and modifying and adding definitions of terms.

The extensive consultation FEMA conducted with tribal governments in the development of the Tribal Declaration Pilot Guidance was not only valuable in informing what the pilot would look like, but also was invaluable to improving our understanding of the needs and unique characteristics of Indian Country. Additionally, it serves as a good example of FEMA's commitment to improving our relationships with tribal governments.

Additional Ongoing Initiatives to Support Tribal Governments

The Federal Insurance and Mitigation Administration (FIMA) supports tribal governments by providing direct assistance and support in the development of FEMA approved Hazard Mitigation Plans and guidance in the development of projects for Hazard Mitigation Assistance (HMA) grants. Hazard mitigation planning enables tribal governments to identify risks and vulnerabilities associated with natural disasters, and develop long-term strategies for protecting people and property from future hazard events. FIMA currently uses regional and headquarter resources to provide outreach and technical assistance to tribal governments in support of these activities. FIMA developed guidance documents, outreach materials and provided training opportunities to educate tribal governments in developing hazard mitigation plans and grant applications, and provided technical assistance to tribal governments applying for, and developing HMA Grants for projects including development of hazard mitigation plans. FIMA also developed resources to assist tribal governments with accessing the eGrants System, and applying directly to FEMA for HMA Grants. In the past two years a portion of the Pre-Disaster Mitigation Grant funds have been set-aside for tribal applications. Tribal nations occupy three of the ten non-FEMA positions on the External Stakeholders Working Group that was formed to increase engagement and transparency with external (non-federal) partners.

In 2016, FIMA conducted tribal consultation on the Tribal Mitigation Planning Guidance that guides agency officials in the interpretation of regulatory requirements in their review and approval of tribal mitigation plans. The underlying regulatory requirements for tribal mitigation planning in 44 CFR Part 201 have not changed. The goal of this update was to simplify and streamline the document, introduce a set of Guiding Principles for Tribal Mitigation Plan Review, and to improve alignment with similar state and local guidance on mitigation planning.

Conclusion

The development and update of FEMA's Tribal Policy, Tribal Consultation Policy, and Tribal Declaration Pilot Guidance shows just part of our commitment to supporting federally recognized tribal governments in their preparation for, protection against, mitigation of, response to, and recovery from all hazards and disasters. The agency continues to seek feedback from our tribal partners and to improve how we can engage and work with them.

We look forward to our continued collaboration to further support tribal governments as they build their emergency management capabilities. Thank you.

The CHAIRMAN. Thank you, Mr. Amparo.

It is my understanding your opening remarks will cover both yourself and Mr. Booth. Mr. Booth, did you have anything to add?

Mr. BOOTH. Yes, sir.

Good afternoon, Chairman Hoeven and Vice Chairman Udall.

I fully support everything that Mr. Amparo has said. I look forward to any questions this Committee may have.

The CHAIRMAN. Thank you.

Next is the Honorable Russell Begaye.

STATEMENT OF HON. RUSSELL BEGAYE, PRESIDENT, NAVAJO NATION

Mr. BEGAYE. Thank you, Chairman. Also, congratulations for taking on this important position for Indian Nations across America. Senator Udall, thank you for assuming that responsibility as Vice Chair of this important Committee.

I am Russell Begaye, President of the Navajo Nation. First, I want to talk about the Gold Kind Mine spill.

On August 5, we saw the river that feeds into our Nation turn yellow as orange juice. It passed the City of Durango. I asked that all of our irrigation systems be cut off to all of our farmland on our Nation. The river runs 200 miles on the Nation so we immediately cut off the source that would contaminate our land, our river and our water.

That was done and we had 200 Navajo Nation employees and volunteers assist in the response but no FEMA employee was on the ground with our people that responded.

On October 2, 2015, we declared an emergency. We made an application to FEMA. FEMA denied us 18 days later on October 20, 2015. In its denial, FEMA said, "The vast majority of the response and recovery efforts for this event fall under the authorities of other Federal agencies."

I met with then Secretary Vilsack from USDA who was willing to help. I met with the Secretary of Health and Human Services. They were willing to come and assist us through the HHS facilities but both of them were told not to get involved with this disaster because they were not the lead agency.

EPA told these Federal agencies not to assist the Navajo Nation because EPA was the lead agency for this. Because of that, USDA, HHS and other Federal agencies did not come alongside the Navajo Nation to help us.

That needs to change because anytime disasters occur, all Federal agencies should use their resources to help Indian tribes like the Navajo Nation in the Gold King Mine spill with their disaster. If that had happened, I know that today farmers would be farming their land. Now they are reluctant to open up the water system because they feel the contaminants are still in the river, still on the banks, still in river banks and the river beds.

To this day, a lot of farmers are reluctant to use the water source. That is the livelihood of our farmers. Not a single farmer to date has been compensated for their loss. We are saying look at the policy. Let all Federal agencies be released to help in any disaster situation.

We would also like to say that because of the resources we have, we are always stretched thin. I urge Congress to review FEMA's funding for tribes so that our people can be better served in event of a disaster.

When you compare this to the BP oil spill, why did FEMA and other Federal agencies engage in that situation, yet shy away from the Gold King Mine spill? EPA is the only one that came and monitored and looked at the river but FEMA was not there because we believe they were told to back off because EPA was the lead agency.

Also, on August 3 through August 5, 2016, the evening of August 3, I was given a call and told that there was a flood coming through the Town of Shiprock. Homes were being washed away and vehicles were floating down the river. A huge disaster took place in the City of Shiprock.

Again we submitted an application to FEMA declaring a major disaster on August 21, 2016. On October 12, 2016, FEMA denied our application because FEMA determined that "The impact to individuals and households from this event was not of such severity and magnitude to warrant supplemental Federal disaster assistance."

We are saying when is it disastrous enough for FEMA to come and help? In this case, these homes were washed away and the vehicles were hanging off the trees two or three days later.

We are asking and appealing that more details about the impact and factors applied by FEMA for individual assistance be clarified. FEMA again denied the appeal we made by simply reaffirming their original conclusion.

FEMA's response was short and general and did not explain how they reached the decision. We are saying we need more guidance and clarity from FEMA when they deny assistance to Indian tribes which encounter disasters.

Thank you.

[The prepared statement of Mr. Begaye follows:]

PREPARED STATEMENT OF HON. RUSSELL BEGAYE, PRESIDENT, NAVAJO NATION

Yá'át'ééh Chairman Hoeven, Ranking Member Udall, and Members of the Committee. My name is Russell Begaye. I am the elected President of the Navajo Nation. Thank you for this opportunity to present testimony to discuss the Navajo Nation's experience in working with Federal Emergency Management Agency (FEMA). I want to talk about two request for declarations that we worked on during my administration: a request for emergency declaration relating to the Gold King Mine spill in August 2015 and a request for a major disaster declaration concerning the Shiprock Flooding that occurred in August of 2016. Unfortunately, both of these requests for declarations were denied. We hope to provide testimony that will prevent tribes in similar situations from being denied federal emergency management resources in times of need.

Gold King Mine, August 2015

As this Committee is aware, on August 5, 2015, the U.S. Environmental Protection Agency (USEPA) and its contractors triggered a release of at least three million gallons of toxic mine waste in the waters directly upstream of the Navajo Nation. The toxic waste flowed into the Animas River and the San Juan River. The San Juan River runs approximately 250 miles along the northern border of the Navajo Nation. Thirteen Navajo Chapters were affected. Upon notice of the spill, the Navajo Nation took action immediately to shut down all intakes into the Shiprock, Upper Fruitland-Cambridge and Hogback irrigation canal systems. The Navajo Nation Department of Emergency Management ("DEM") identified livestock watering points in the affected area. Our teams worked with the BIA to haul water and set up water tanks at these watering points. The Navajo Nation DEM provided ranchers and farmers information about safe water intake for livestock and for preserving crop fields. The Navajo Nation's EPA monitored water quality at eleven strategic points along the San Juan River. The Nation's DEM activated the Emergency Operations Center (EOC) to coordinate the Nation's response to this toxic spill. In all, approximately 200 Navajo Nation DEM and Navajo EPA employees and volunteers assisted in the response to this disastrous federal EPA-triggered spill. No federal FEMA employees were ever on the ground.

The Nation submitted its FEMA application for an emergency application on October 2, 2015. FEMA notified the Nation on October 20, 2015 that it denied our application for an emergency declaration. FEMA's justification for the denial was that the agency determined that "the vast majority of the response and recovery efforts for this event fall under the authorities of other federal agencies." The "other federal agency" referred to by FEMA was the USEPA, the agency responsible for causing the emergency situation, and with a strong self-interest in minimizing the response in order to minimize potential liability for its actions. Despite this strong conflict of interest, the Obama administration designated USEPA as the lead federal agency for spill response. We believe the designation of the USEPA as the lead agency blocked assistance from other federal agencies including FEMA and the U.S. Department of Agriculture (USDA). For example, in discussions with FEMA staff, we were informed that FEMA's "federal mission" does not include livestock and crop fields, and livestock and crop fields were the most affected by the toxic spill. FEMA staff also informed us that USDA assistance for livestock and crop fields are provided under major disaster declarations, not under emergency declarations. When we reached out to the USDA we were informed their regulations prohibited them from assisting us here because the livestock and crop fields were impacted by an emergency, not a major disaster. As you know, the USEPA recently declared that they are not legally responsible for the spill—just days before the Obama administration left office. The bottom line is that the USEPA caused this spill, and our Navajo people who have suffered greatly as a result of the spill have yet to be compensated for their damages.

In addition to the above roadblocks, we were also informed that FEMA does not generally get involved in emergency assistance when an actual or potentially liable party is involved, as was the case with the Gold King Mine spill.

In regards to FEMA and other agencies lack of involvement in the Gold King Mine spill, we ask whether FEMA applies this policy selectively because it is our understanding that FEMA provided assistance during the BP oil spill that occurred in the Gulf of Mexico where many federal departments became involved and there were liable parties. Why did President Obama's FEMA engage in the BP-caused Gulf of Mexico spill, yet shy away from the USEPA-caused Gold King Mine spill? We ask the Committee to explore the difference in assistance and response between these two cases.

FEMA's denial of an emergency declaration also effectively denied the Nation assistance for its people through counseling services. We received many requests from the local chapters and individuals for counseling services. We would have applied for counseling services assistance from the U.S. Department of Health and Human Services (DHHS) for those affected by the spill as well as responders to the spill. However, when we requested this assistance from DHHS, it informed us that it can only provide this service if an emergency declaration is made and approved by FEMA. We request this policy be reviewed—our people should not be denied access to federal counseling services that would normally have been available under different political circumstances.

Our Navajo DEM is made up of only 3 employees. When a disaster occurs, they must take the lead in organizing the response. This is a lot of work and yet at the same time, they have to make assessments, develop all the documentation, and submit all the required documents to FEMA. As such, our resources are stretched thin. Comparable State emergency departments are made up of 50 or more people. I imagine that a smaller Tribe than the Navajo Nation, who has limited or no resources will have even greater difficulty in getting any type of declaration approved by FEMA. I therefore urge Congress to review FEMA funding for Tribes so that our people can be better served in the event of a disaster. Our emergency response teams should have the same resources as State teams, and Congress can help ensure this parity.

Because the USEPA caused this spill, it effectively prevented FEMA from taking the lead and engaging with the Navajo Nation. The USEPA then denied our claims a year-and-a-half after the spill and only days before the Obama administration left office. I find it appalling that a federal agency can cause a spill, testify before this Committee that it takes full responsibility, then prevent FEMA from engaging, then finally deny liability. This should never be allowed to happen again.

Shiprock Flooding, August 2016

From August 3–5, 2016, flooding occurred in northwest Shiprock, New Mexico on the Navajo reservation. Three hours after the rainstorm reached its peak, residents in the affected area began calling public rescue agencies who responded immediately. Individuals and families were evacuated to the Shiprock Chapter ("Chapter") House. Red Cross had supplies and bedding set up in the Chapter House. The local emergency response team, entitled the Shiprock ALERT Team, set up a command post in the Chapter House. DEM provided technical assistance to the Shiprock ALERT Team. In the early morning of August 6th, breakers and water lines were shut down; roads were cleared of flood debris so that residents and rescuers could travel in and out of the area. A loader and bar screen was used to clear flood debris from the demolished houses. Trash bins were donated so that debris could be quickly removed, thus reducing risks to public health. Donations were being continuously received at the Chapter and distributed to affected residents. Temporary housing was found for those whose homes had washed away. Public meetings were held at the Chapter House to keep the community regularly informed. The Nation's Division of Health staff assisted affected residents by providing them with safety and health information and monitoring them for days.

The primary area where flooding occurred was approximately three square miles. Twenty-seven homes were affected and all were surveyed for damage by DEM and FEMA. Ten were deemed to be affected but habitable, two had minor damage and five sustained major damage. Ten homes were destroyed. Eleven vehicles were destroyed and five of these washed away. The damage to the affected families was documented and estimated at $967,516. Five months after the flooding seven families have been re-settled, nine families continue living in temporary homes, three have been provided trailers by the Navajo Nation, one person is homeless, one family purchased their own home, and one family is renovating their home to make it habitable.

The Navajo Nation submitted its FEMA major disaster declaration application on September 21, 2016. On October 12, 2016, FEMA denied our application because FEMA "determined that the impact to individuals and households from this event was not of such severity and magnitude as to warrant supplemental federal disaster assistance." The Nation appealed FEMA's denial on November 9, 2016. Our appeal emphasized the individual assistance factors applied by FEMA pursuant to 44 CFR 206.48(b): (1) concentration of damages, (2) trauma, (3) special populations, (4) voluntary agency assistance, and (5) insurance. [1] On November 28, 2016, FEMA notified the Nation that its appeal was denied. The denial simply reaffirmed FEMA's original conclusion that the "impact to individuals and households from this event is not of the severity and magnitude as to warrant supplemental federal assistance."

The original FEMA denial stated only that the impact to the individuals and families was not severe enough and the magnitude was not sufficient enough. In our appeal, we gave more details about the impact experienced by the affected individuals and families in accordance with the factors applied by FEMA for individual assistance. Nonetheless, FEMA denied our appeal on the same basis of insufficient severity and magnitude.

The Nation requests clearer guidance from FEMA to Indian tribes who apply for individual assistance. Because FEMA did not explain how and why it reached the conclusion that it did, we can only speculate about the basis of their conclusion with questions such as the following. Was the 3 square-mile area not of sufficient magnitude? Given the census population numbers we included for the Shiprock community, were 21 families not sufficient to warrant a declaration? Were the estimated total damage costs of $967,516 not severe enough or of sufficient magnitude? The Nation does not know what thresholds apply under each factor that FEMA considers in deciding whether a major disaster event qualifies for federal assistance. In addition, the Nation wonders whether the scope of the disaster response might have worked against a declaration decision because the locally-based Shiprock ALERT Team functioned as the primary responder, not the Nation's DEM. Shiprock ALERT Team was right there in the community and could respond immediately and coordinate services for rescue, repair, and aid. Because the affected area was a residential area, the flooding did not impact any government operations or facilities. This experience with unclear guidance from FEMA about its individual assistance determinations leads us to request that FEMA provide clear guidance for Indian tribes with respect to applications for individual assistance.

The Nation also recommends that FEMA consider a class of disaster relief that would allow for assistance for individuals who have disaster damages that are localized in scope even if tribal government functions and facilities are not affected. Given the limited resources of all types for Indian tribes, even a localized disaster event will greatly challenge the internal resources of most Indian tribes.

Other Declarations

Prior to my Presidency, there were two other Navajo Nation declarations approved by FEMA. One declaration was for a freeze that occurred across the Navajo Nation around December 2012 to January 2013. The Nation had filed a request for a major disaster declaration and FEMA approved the declaration. This declaration was filed shortly after the Stafford Act was changed to allow Indian tribes to file

---

[1] The 6th factor applies primarily to states.

declarations for themselves rather than go through the state. Navajo was one of the first few tribes to file pursuant to this new law.

The other declaration was made as a result of severe storms, flooding and mudslides that occurred in New Mexico from July through September of 2013, but this assistance did not come from Navajo's own declaration. Initially, from our understanding, Navajo was denied assistance from FEMA because the cumulative amount of Navajo's documented damages did not exceed the $1 million threshold. In the alternative, the Nation filed as a subgrantee of the State of New Mexico under their declaration since their cumulative damages would then exceed the $1 million threshold. The tribal threshold has since been reduced to $250,000, which now makes it easier for tribes to receive assistance.

If you need further information on these declarations, we can provide it upon your request.

Conclusion

FEMA recently published a Tribal Declarations Pilot Guidance dated January 2017. We provided comments to the draft of this guidance. However, at this time, we are working to see if any of our comments were incorporated into that Guidance. When the flooding and the Gold King Mine spill occurred, we did not have this guidance and we had to rely on specialized expertise and navigate the complex maze of federal regulations. Since it is in the pilot phase, we shall see how this will help us out in the future.

The Nation places a spotlight on the difficulties Indian tribes confront when attempting to apply for emergency declaration assistance, especially when federal guidelines and regulations require criteria that do not apply to an emergency event such as the toxic spill that contaminated the San Juan River and yet caused damage to vitally important tribal resources. As a result, many of the individual farmers and ranchers affected by the toxic spill remain uncompensated almost two years after the event. The fact that farmers have not been compensated for their EPA-caused losses and the fact that FEMA was prevented from engaging is absolutely unacceptable. I commend this Committee for focusing on tribes' difficulties in obtaining disaster assistance from the Federal Government.

The CHAIRMAN. Thank you, President Begaye.

We will now turn to Governor Chavarria.

STATEMENT OF HON. J. MICHAEL CHAVARRIA, GOVERNOR, PUEBLO OF SANTA CLARA

Mr. CHAVARRIA. [Greeting in native tongue.]

Out of respect, Mr. Chairman, Vice Chairman and members of the Committee, my name is Michael Chavarria, Governor for Santa Clara Pueblo.

In my native Santa Clara, I just asked the Chairman, out of respect, to speak on behalf of my Pueblo in Santa Clara and for an invitation to testify this afternoon before this Committee.

In the last 20 years, the Santa Clara Pueblo has faced and overcome numerous natural disasters. In 2011, as Vice Chairman, I mentioned we were devastated with the Las Conchas fire.

The fire caused damage to our forests and lands which is our pharmacy. The Santa Clara Creek is a biological classroom. Most of our Santa Clara Canyon, which is our spiritual sanctuary, has a 25.9 mile burn scar across our traditional lands. The burn scar destabilized the land and left our community vulnerable to flashfloods and mudslides.

While FEMA and other Federal agencies have undertaken significant efforts to protect our people and our lands, that threat still remains. Our lands remain unstable and our prone to the imminent threat of flooding.

However, we are thankful to those Federal agencies for coming to our aid and continue to partner for the resilience of flooding for Santa Clara Pueblo.

As mentioned, we had five presidential disaster declarations. We have two or three as a sub-grantee to the State of New Mexico and as Stafford amendments were made, we have two direct disaster declarations for Santa Clara Pueblo.

There are serious financial considerations in choosing whether to proceed as a sub-grantee or as a direct grantee. As a sub-grantee to the State, we are responsible for 12.5 percent of that cost. However as a direct grantee, we are obligated to meet 25 percent of that cost while the Federal Government through FEMA covers the remaining 75 percent.

With five presidential disaster declarations, Santa Clara has been responsible for tens of millions of dollars in cost sharing matches which has placed a tremendous burden on our already limited tribal budgets and has taken away from other social programs for our elders and children.

One of the things I have recommended is adjusting the cost share thresholds to be more responsive to the financial needs of the tribe. Santa Clara took that opportunity by writing to Mr. Tony Robinson, Regional Administrator on September 26, 2014 pursuant to 44 CFR Subsection 206.47 about a reduction in the local cost share. "Yes, this request could be authorized but must be approved by the President."

With this, we are approved at a 10 percent cost share reduction. This is very vital because we are not wealthy financially. However, we are wealthy with our traditions, our culture and our religion. An important thing is our Native language which is the glue that holds together our culture and traditions.

Because the devastation was so huge in November 2013, Santa Clara became the first tribal government to request and receive disaster recovery assistance under the National Disaster Recovery Framework, the NDRF.

The NDRF is used to create a comprehensive federally-led strategy to the build the community's resiliency to future flooding. The National Disaster Recovery Framework incorporates a recovery support strategy which enables the tribes to maximize their resources by enabling the tribes to coordinate with Federal, State and non-governmental organizations through a systematic approach that is mutually beneficial. Most importantly, it respects our sovereignty.

I have submitted a written statement for this hearing. It contains the background of the fire, the impacts and continued threats to our existence as Santa Clara Pueblo. Most important is a graph that was provided by the Corps of Engineers that shows on any given day, we face a 100-year flood event.

Pre-fire, it was 5,000 cubic feet per second. Because no more vegetation was there, we are now prone to a 21,000 cubic feet per second flood event within our canyon because of the altered hydrology.

This is very important. Five minutes is not really enough time to go into full detail about our challenges. However, I would like to recommend that we support Stafford amendments which promote self determination and better reflect the unique government-to-government relationship that exists between FEMA and tribal nations.

Second, we recommend the creation of a BIA emergency response fund that will be equipped to provide tribes with emergency funding to address short and long term disaster recovery and prevention efforts.

Third, we also recommend additional funding for effective fire prevention treatment such as fuel breaks, hazardous fuel reduction projects which could then provide our lands with greater protection and reduce the need for extensive costly fire suppression efforts.

Fourth, we support the expansion of land management programs such as the Tribal Forest Protection Act that empowers tribal governments to act as caretakers of those Federal lands adjacent to our reservation and partnering the tribes to protect the trust resources is very vital.

Finally, we support the FEMA Tribal Declaration Pilot Guidance as a valuable addition to the Federal toolbox. It reflects the diverse voices of Indian country including our own and is responsive to our concerns.

Thank you, Mr. Chairman and members of the Committee. I now stand for any questions you may have at this time.

[The prepared statement of Mr. Chavarria follows:]

PREPARED STATEMENT OF HON. J. MICHAEL CHAVARRIA, GOVERNOR, PUEBLO OF SANTA CLARA

Thank you Chairman Hoeven, Vice Chairman Udall, and members of the Committee for this opportunity to provide testimony on the critically important topic of natural disasters in Indian Country. Our Pueblo thanks you for your dedicated work on behalf of Indian tribes across the nation, particularly in the southwest.

My name is J. Michael Chavarria and I am the Governor of the Santa Clara Pueblo, located in north-central New Mexico. Because of wildfires and subsequent intense flooding, the Santa Clara Pueblo has had five Presidential Disaster Declarations (or PDDs) in the last five years. Indeed, in a report issued after the fire, the U.S. Army Corps of Engineers observed, "*The Village of Santa Clara Pueblo is in imminent threat of large damaging floods with extreme life safety risk.*" My testimony shares our experience with disaster relief and its impacts, as well as the lessons we have learned in overcoming challenges related to emergency management. It concludes with our top five recommendations for improving FEMA's relationship with Indian tribes. Thank you.

Background on the Las Conchas Fire and its Impact

In the summer of 2011, the Santa Clara Pueblo was devastated by the Las Conchas Fire, which was then the largest wildfire in New Mexico history. We estimate that over 16,000 acres of our forestlands were burned, which—when combined with the lands we lost in the Oso Complex Fire of 1998 and the Cerro Grande Fire of 2000—has resulted in the destruction of 80% of our forests and a huge part of our cultural heritage. None of the four fires we have faced in the past decade have originated on our lands, yet we have suffered the repeated and severe consequences of these natural disasters.

Outside of our current reservation, the Las Conchas fire burned thousands of additional acres of our traditional lands—including the lands of our origin, the P'opii Khanu, which are the forested headwaters of the Santa Clara Creek. The Santa Clara Creek drains the east side of the Jemez Mountains, delivering its waters to the Rio Grande near Española, NM. The Pueblo owns almost the entire watershed, and our tribal village is located on the Creek's alluvial fan, where the Creek joins the Rio Grande.

The Las Conchas fire scorched the Creek's upper watershed and most of the Santa Clara Canyon, leaving a 25.9 mile burn scar in its wake. A burn scar refers to land that has been charred and stripped of all vegetation by a wildfire. Because the land is devoid of vegetation, no root systems remain in place to secure the land. As a result, the land is vulnerable to flash floods and mudslides. Our Pueblo has experienced severe flash flooding since the fire.

All five of the Pueblo's Presidential Disaster Declarations have involved infrastructure damage stemming from catastrophic flash floods. Flooding has wiped out existing water control structures within the canyon, destroyed once-pristine native cutthroat fish habitat, impacted roads, taken away culverts, and damaged the traditional cultural properties of our sanctuary.

Impacts. Santa Clara has had five Presidential Disaster Declarations: three by the request of the State of New Mexico and two by the Pueblo after the Stafford Act was amended. Overall, the ability to directly request Presidential Disaster Declarations has given Santa Clara Pueblo greater control over our own disaster relief efforts. Further, implementation of FEMA's National Disaster Recovery Framework (NDRF), which facilitates inter-agency collaboration, has been helpful to Santa Clara in assuring a comprehensive and coordinated effort among the federal family.

However, despite the hard work of many dedicated agency staff members, current laws and regulations regarding disaster relief remain a product of a different time, with the effect of slowing the delivery of critically needed resources. The flood disaster relief framework remains broadly tailored to one-time floods on the Mississippi River and, thus, is focused on short-term efforts (and this not only refers to funding, but to how each contract is written and the expectations of the implementing policies). Given the realities of life in the southwestern United States and the increasing effects of climate change, disaster relief policies must be shifted to focus on long-term responses to challenges such as Santa Clara's post-fire, periodic flooding, which will remain a hazard to our well-being for perhaps a decade as the Santa Clara Canyon slowly recovers. Although significant progress has been made, more work remains to be done to ensure effective responses to natural disasters in Indian Country.

Continued Threat of Catastrophic Floods. Because of the altered hydrology and geomorphic changes to the land, the Pueblo remains in danger of a catastrophic flood, but that danger has been substantially mitigated by the construction of three large gabion structures in the canyon, as well as other water control structures and actions. The severity of the burn scar has led to a dramatic reduction in infiltration rates in the affected area. This has resulted in a four-to-eight-fold increase in runoff and sediment/debris flow along the Creek, substantially increasing the potential for widespread damage. Although it was originally thought that a full-scale dam would be necessary in the canyon, after technological review demonstrated the extraordinary difficulty of building such a structure, the next alternative was the gabion structures.

The graph below contains data from the U.S. Army Corps of Engineers on the hydrology of the Santa Clara Creek pre- and post-fire. As the graph indicates, the worst-case scenario would be a storm of such force that it is generally considered to happen once every 100 years. For the Rio Grande Confluence, such a storm would have flooded 5,640 cubic feet per second (cfs) pre-fire and now, post-fire, would flood 21,450 cfs.

Table 1: Flow Results Summary (cubic feet per second, cfs) Source: Fire Altered Hydrology for Santa Clara Creek/ USACE Technical Assistance Report				
LOCATION	CONDITION	50% CHANCE (2-YR)	10% CHANCE (10-YR)	1% CHANCE (100-YR)
Santa Clara Creek at Dip Crossing	Pre-fire	300	1,900	5,000
Santa Clara Creek at Rio Grande Confluence (Outlet)	Pre-fire	350	2,260	5,640

<u>**Lessons from the Santa Clara's Disaster Relief Experiences**</u>

Experience as a Sub- and Direct Grantee. Santa Clara Pueblo has experience as both a sub-grantee and direct grantee of Presidential Disaster Declarations. As the Committee is aware, until recently, Presidential Disaster Declarations could only be requested through the states. For tribes, securing a state request for a Presidential Disaster Declaration could be difficult. New Mexico, however, did not fit that mold and it requested two such declarations on behalf of Santa Clara Pueblo. Unfortunately, in those instances it still took up to a year for the Pueblo to receive the requested disaster relief funds from the State, hampering our ability to provide urgently needed immediate relief.

Amendments to the Stafford Act now allow tribes to directly request Presidential Disaster Declarations. The ability to become direct-grantees has given Santa Clara Pueblo greater ability to direct its own disaster relief efforts.

National Disaster Recovery Framework (NDRF). The NDRF has been enormously helpful in coordinating agency responses and providing a more collaborative and effective approach to disaster recovery. In November 2013, Santa Clara Pueblo became the first tribal government to request and receive federal disaster recovery assistance under the National Disaster Recovery Framework (NDRF). FEMA used the NDRF to create a comprehensive federally□led strategy for the Pueblo to identify all possible actions that would build the community's resiliency to future flooding. The NDRF provided the Pueblo with an opportunity to effectively develop recovery strategies for our respective areas. This support system enabled FEMA to extend their resources to the Pueblo and helped to define a series of important core recovery principles, namely:

- Roles and responsibilities of recovery coordinators and other stakeholders;
- A coordinating structure that facilitates communication and collaboration among all stakeholders;
- Guidance documents for pre- and post-disaster recovery planning; and
- The overall process by which communities can capitalize on opportunities to rebuild in stronger, smarter and safer ways following a disaster.

Transitioning Best Practices to Support the NDRF. After the Las Conchas fire, Santa Clara Pueblo recognized the potential for flood impacts on downstream resources and our tribal village. Tribal representatives contacted the southwest Tri-Regional Burn Area Emergency Response (BAER) coordinator and the National Interagency Fire Center (NIFC) to request assistance with emergency post-fire stabilization planning. BAER team members worked with the Pueblo to prescribe and implement treatments in an effort to protect life and property from future flooding.

Subject matter experts have been instrumental in coordinating federal resources to assist the Pueblo in our recovery efforts. During conversations with the Pueblo as part of the NDRF process, an approach was agreed upon to leverage other federal agency staff engaged in the workgroup and incorporate them into the recovery planning process through FEMA's Mission Assignment process. This approach had the two-fold benefit of establishing inter-agency and federal-tribal relationships and effectively integrating disciplines for a common purpose.

The Las Conchas Fire Rehabilitation Workgroup subsequently transitioned to the Las Conchas Team. It was in this support system where Santa Clara Pueblo began to utilize resources from partnering agencies, such as the Recovery Support Strategy (RSS), and investing in building the Pueblo's internal response capacity.

Recovery Support Strategy (RSS). The Recovery Support Strategy is a dynamic, interactive document that provides federal and tribal partners with a detailed vision to help guide the recovery support. The RSS uses Recovery Support Functions to coordinate key areas of national assistance during the NRDF process. Each Recovery Support Function is managed by a Coordinating Agency, which serves to coordinate a range of federal agency resources. The RSS is continually revised as engagement with tribal officials progresses, and as the recovery objectives and priorities of the Santa Clara Pueblo are further refined.

The RSS identifies objectives and support actions; member agencies needed to implement the actions and Recovery Support Functions; and the necessary resources to achieve the recovery objectives so that the Santa Clara Pueblo will be more resilient in the face of future disasters. Given the focused nature of impacts within the canyon and riparian channel, it was decided that a full complement of the Recovery Support Functions would not be required in support of Santa Clara Pueblo, but should instead focus on: (a) community planning and capacity building; (b) watershed stabilization; and (c) natural and cultural resource protection. We have made significant progress in addressing these areas through a targeted, phased-action approach. In terms of the general RSS, our recovery themes focused on the following:

(i) Focus initially on short-term actions to protect the Village and its people from imminent threats of flooding.

(ii) Continue to leverage federal and state interagency partnerships and technical support.
(iii) Regularly assess the natural restoration of the Santa Clara Canyon to strategically plan its long-term recovery in a way that balances the natural recovery processes with man-made designs.
(iv) Assess all recommended projects for both feasibility and realism to ensure projects are compatible with the Pueblo's long-term management capacity.
(v) Assure all NDRF partner actions are respectful of Santa Clara's culture and sovereignty.

Through the support of the NDRF and RSS, Santa Clara Pueblo was able to establish a foundation that allows the Pueblo to mold the Framework to fit the Pueblo's unique needs and created a strategic approach to recovery. The RSS has allowed us to prioritize recovery efforts and to help identify agencies to assist us through support from their respective agencies. This has broadened our span of financial resources as well as strengthened collaboration among our federal, state and non-governmental partners.

Tribal Declarations Pilot Guidance. FEMA has consulted with tribal governments to discuss the implementation of direct tribal declarations. Through conference calls, participation in in-person meetings, and written submissions, FEMA heard from tribal leaders, tribal, state and local emergency managers, and other interested participants about how to process declaration requests from tribal governments. Participants also provided recommendations on how FEMA should evaluate requests and make recommendations to the President about whether to grant declarations for impacted tribes. FEMA considered all of this input in the development of this draft guidance.

Participants provided examples of unique circumstances that affect tribal governments, such as extreme remoteness, high unemployment, and the tribal governments' various decision-making structures. Some raised concerns that tribal governments have limited fiscal and staffing capacities even in non-disaster times, which may affect their ability to administer disaster assistance and cover non-federal cost shares. In addition, participants expressed concern about how FEMA would define the incident area and tribal lands for declaration purposes. FEMA also received many comments on the evaluation criteria for Individual and Public Assistance requests and cost share adjustment requests. Finally, tribal officials requested additional consultation and technical assistance to better understand the requirements and implications of direct declarations.

This guidance will be a tool that outlines FEMA's commitment to collaborate with tribes on disaster recovery and prevention efforts. It allows FEMA to actively engage in developing ways to better support tribes by providing critical training and technical services. FEMA Region VI has been a great partner in helping support Santa Clara Pueblo through the process of obtaining and effectively managing our Tribal Declaration.

Overcoming Challenges. The direct grantee process, however, is not without its challenges. It is a new process, and Santa Clara Pueblo has been the first tribe to utilize it in FEMA Region VI. For both the Pueblo and the Region, there is a lot of learning that has to take place. We have been going through that learning process with FEMA and in many ways we feel like we are pathfinders for other tribes, should they be so unfortunate as to face the difficulties we have learned to overcome. The support from FEMA Region VI allowed Santa Clara Pueblo to have access to immediate resources to manage two separate disaster situations for which we sought direct Tribal

Declarations.

As a sub-grantee, receiving funds through the State, the Pueblo must meet a cost-share match of 12.5% while the State has the burden of administering the grant on our behalf. The cost-share match of a direct grantee is 25%, although this can be lowered to 10% once a per capita threshold is met. Santa Clara Pueblo recognizes the barriers the cost-match may pose to tribes and understands how tribes may be reluctant to seek a Tribal Disaster Declaration as a result.

As a small tribe ourselves, our five Presidential Disaster Declarations (PDDs) have been a significant financial burden. The matching funds requirement has drained the Pueblo's financials resources. Due to these tremendous financial responsibilities, the Pueblo has requested that FEMA combine the five PDDs into one so that the Pueblo is in a better position to meet the financial cost share responsibilities. This would also enable the Pueblo to reach the 90/10 cost-share level using the per capita figures. Right now, we are only able to meet that threshold on one PDD while the others are variously administered at 12.5% and 25% cost-share levels. Such variations in financial responsibilities are challenges we must be aware of so as a tribal government to properly allocate funds and move forward with our obligations.

Furthermore, there are variations in administrative cost responsibilities for tribes under a PDD. As a direct grantee the Pueblo is responsible for associated administrative costs, although we do receive 3.37% in administrative funding from FEMA. As a sub grantee, however, funding for management costs is often determined by the State and there is not a guarantee that the tribe will receive any financial support for those costs. This places a significant burden on tribes because they often lack the financial resources to support additional staff and emergency services. Tribes may also face challenges in meeting the $1 million FEMA threshold. This threshold should be revised to coincide with tribes' financial resources and capacities, and tribal consortiums should be able to apply for relief in order to meet this threshold.

Additionally, we have seen smaller projects receive quick funding responses from FEMA, while larger projects remain mired in time-consuming quality assurance and quality control processes. While clearly important, these processes greatly lengthen the review time during a period when time is of essence in preventing or mitigating a natural disaster. For Santa Clara Pueblo, as we enter the New Mexico monsoon season, we spend every day scanning the skies and read the weather reports, fearing the worst and praying for the best. Receiving funds to support recovery efforts prior to the seasonal impacts of monsoons is imperative in breaking the cycle of continued damage. As our PDD experiences demonstrate, in emergencies project implementation is crucial to protecting lives, securing communities, and preventing repeated damage to key infrastructure.

Finally, the administrative responsibility that comes along with being a direct grantee has challenged the Pueblo. We certainly have proven that we have the administrative capability to administer these programs, but we had to learn through trial and error. As the changes to the Stafford Act allowing tribes to request direct declarations are promulgated, FEMA may best be served by implementing a training program that better communicates the regulatory requirements associated with being a direct grantee. This would better enable tribes to make informed decisions regarding FEMA assistance and would also allow FEMA to familiarize itself with the diverse capabilities of tribal governments.

As the first tribe in Region 6 to receive direct funding, we know that we are involved in a learning process with our federal partners. Training and capacity building is needed on both sides of the federal–tribal partnership. Tribes need additional training and technical assistance to administer funds successfully and our federal partners could benefit from allowing tribes to conduct training for tribal liaisons to help them become more familiar with working with tribal governments. Together we can work together to build our mutual capacities and identify areas in which disaster relief policy can be adapted to address the unique emergency service needs of Indian Country. In light of these considerations, we therefore recommend the following.

<u>Recommendations</u>

1. **Emergency Response Fund.** Our experiences with disaster relief highlight the need for tribes to receive assistance as soon as possible following a natural disaster. Empowering tribes to directly request a Presidential Disaster Declaration can be helpful, but standing alone it does not fully address the need for quick funding. For this reason, we recommend the creation of a BIA Emergency Response Fund. The idea behind this fund would be for the BIA to have readily at hand significant funding that can be deployed as necessary to address short- and long-term disaster recovery and disaster mitigation needs.

2. **Support for the FEMA Tribal Guidance Document.** FEMA developed the Tribal Declarations Pilot Guidance after several rounds of consultation with tribal governments over the course of more than three years. The document reflects the diverse voices of tribal leaders and emergency management officials, among others, and is responsive to their concerns. We support the FEMA Tribal Guidance Document as a tool to be used alongside the NRDF and RSS.

3. **Maintenance of the Stafford Act Amendments.** The Stafford Act amendments allow tribal governments the choice to either request an emergency/major disaster declaration independently of a state or to seek disaster assistance through a state declaration. The amended Stafford Act better reflects the sovereignty of tribal governments and acknowledges FEMA's government-to-government relationship with tribal governments. It also promotes tribal self-determination by allowing tribal governments to determine for themselves how they want to seek Stafford Act assistance either independently of a state or through a state declaration. We therefore recommend that these amendments be maintained in the event that the Stafford Act is amended in the future.

4. **Appropriate necessary funds for implementation of Forest treatments as identified under the Tribal Forest Protection Act (TFPA).** The TFPA authorizes the secretaries of Agriculture and Interior to give special consideration to tribally-proposed Stewardship Contracting or other projects on Forest Service or BLM land bordering or adjacent to Indian trust land to protect trust resources from fire, disease, and other threats. These stewardship agreements are an important tool for fighting the ever-growing threat of wildfires in the West. Empowering tribal governments as caretakers to protect tribal lands by managing adjacent federal lands is a smart policy. Santa Clara urges the Committee to support the expansion of this program going forward.

5. Additional funding for fire prevention treatments on and off tribal reservations. Santa Clara recommends the consideration of alternative fire prevention land management techniques that would allow tribal grantees to render timely responses to emergencies and reduce the threat of catastrophic fires encroaching upon our trust resources. Huge amounts of funds are used annually for fire suppression treatments while those same funds could be used to implement a variety of effective and relatively low-cost fire *prevention* techniques, such as hazardous fuels reduction and fuel breaks. We therefore recommend additional funding for fire prevention activities to protect tribal and federal lands.

Conclusion. I would like to conclude my remarks by thanking the many individuals that we work with at the Federal Emergency Management Agency, the Army Corps of Engineers, the Bureau of Indian Affairs, the Bureau of Reclamation, the U.S. Department of Agriculture, and others, for the long hours that they have committed to addressing what continues to be an existential threat to the Santa Clara Pueblo. Despite working with laws and regulations that can be cumbersome or designed for very different emergency situations, they continue to show commitment and determination, for which I and my people are truly grateful. There is work to be done and there are significant improvements to be made, but at Santa Clara we have hope that after suffering a terrible loss we can secure the safety of our community in the short-term, as well as its cultural and spiritual integrity and prosperity in the long-term.

Thank you for the opportunity to testify on behalf of this important issue. The Pueblo of Santa Clara looks forward to working with you on addressing these complex needs going forward.

The CHAIRMAN. Thank you, Governor Chavarria.
Now we will turn to Director Desautel.

STATEMENT OF CODY DESAUTEL, NATURAL RESOURCES DIRECTOR, CONFEDERATED TRIBES OF THE COLVILLE RESERVATION

Mr. DESAUTEL. Good afternoon, Chairman Hoeven, Vice Chairman Udall, and members of the Committee. I appreciate the opportunity to testify today.

My name is Cody Desautel and I am the Natural Resources Director for the Confederated Tribes of the Colville Reservation. The tribe appreciates the opportunity and would like to share our important issues and experiences working with FEMA during disasters.

The Colville Reservation covers approximately 1.4 million acres. The reservation is slightly larger than the State of Delaware by area. About half of the tribe's members live on our reservation.

Of the 1.4 million acres, more than 900,000 are forested and of those 900,000 forested acres, over 660,000 our part of our commercial cut base which we rely on for timber production and revenue that supports our tribal government.

I am going to address three issues. The first will be the catastrophic fires we had in 2014 and 2015 and later a windstorm event we had in 2012.

The catastrophic fires are explained in my written statement. In eastern Washington, we saw the worse fire season in the State's history in 2014 and 2015. In 2014, four fires collectively referred to as the Carlton Complex, burned 256,000 acres in communities near the Colville Reservation.

While damage to the Colville Reservation was comparatively small and limited to our inhabited rangeland, our tribal personnel assisted local governments in the suppression and recovery efforts.

The Carlton Complex fire burned more than 300 homes and other structures and affected life and property throughout two watersheds.

In 2015, the Colville Tribes endured the most destructive fire on an Indian reservation in recorded history. The North Star and Okanogan Complex fires collectively burned more than 255,000 acres on the Colville Reservation, nearly 20 percent of the total land base, and approximately one-fourth of the commercial timber land.

Approximately 800 million board feet of timber we think was burned but further inventory work is ongoing to fully assess the damage of that fire season.

The 2015 fires statewide resulted in the deaths of three firefighters, a non-firefighting fatality and 21 injuries, and ultimately burned more than 1 million acres in the State. The Okanogan Complex fire surpassed the 2014 Carlton Complex fire as the largest fire in Washington State history.

2015 marked the first year ever that Washington State officials asked residents to volunteer to assist in fighting wildfires.

For both the 2014 Carlton Complex and the 2015 fires, the President issued PDDs that authorized public assistance for both the Colville Tribes and the affected local governments. In both cases, however, FEMA denied Governor Inslee's requests for assistance for homeowners under FEMA's Individual Assistance Program.

The tribe then submitted its own separate request for Individual Assistance for on-reservation residents. FEMA denied that request as well.

The second point is catastrophic wildfires should be treated differently by FEMA. Neither FEMA nor the Stafford Act adequately addresses the full extent of damage caused by massive, catastrophic wildfires, especially for Indian tribes.

In the next few years to Colville Tribe's single largest task will be replanting trees burned during the 2015 wildfire season. The only dedicated funding source for replanting is BIA funds which are somewhat limited, as I am sure you know. The BIA has a statutory obligation to replant Indian forests but its annual average reforestation budget is approximately $3.4 million. In comparison, the tribe's request for rehabilitation funding was roughly $20 million.

This would cover planting of less than 11,000 acres for all tribes nationwide. I think just in 2015, there was half a million acres of Indian forests burned.

For catastrophic fire events, FEMA should provide immediate assistance for fire suppression, stabilization and landscape rehabilitation. For Indian forestland, FEMA should also provide resources for replanting in light of the United States' trust obligations to reforest Indian forestland.

One approach would be to create a separate disaster declaration category for catastrophic fire events. This concept was included in Title IX of the House-passed Resilient Federal Forests Act of 2015.

As a third point, FEMA should re-examine its criteria to ensure rural tribal communities are treated fairly. One of FEMA's criteria for evaluating requests for individual assistance is concentration of damages.

FEMA has never explained why it denied the Washington State and Colville Tribes' requests for individual assistance for the 2014 or 2015 fires. The tribes believe the fact that much of the damage was widespread over a large geographic area was the primary reason for the denial.

Rural areas like the Colville Reservation are inherently prone to a lower concentration of damages based on population density but often suffer more damage than metropolitan areas. This was the case with the affected residents of the Colville Reservation, many of whom lost access to health care and other essentials due to extended road closures.

Other tribal members lost their livelihoods when cattle and rangeland burned, which are damages that have persisted and will continue long after the fires were extinguished.

The new FEMA Pilot Guidance for Tribal Disaster Declaration did not affect how FEMA applies concentration of damages to tribes. We believe FEMA should amend this guidance to issue new guidance that makes clear that rural Indian tribes will not be denied assistance based on concentration of damages.

This concludes my testimony and I would be happy to answer any questions the Committee may have.

[The prepared statement of Mr. Desautel follows:]

PREPARED STATEMENT OF CODY DESAUTEL, NATURAL RESOURCES DIRECTOR, CONFEDERATED TRIBES OF THE COLVILLE RESERVATION

Good afternoon, Chairman Hoeven, Vice Chairman Udall, and members of the Committee. My name is Cody Desautel and I am the Natural Resources Director for the Confederated Tribes of the Colville Reservation ("Colville Tribes" or the "CCT"). I appreciate the opportunity to testify on improving FEMA's relationship with Indian tribes.

My testimony today will focus on three issues: (1) the impact of three major disasters on the Colville Reservation during the past five years, including two massive wildfires; (2) why catastrophic wildfires should be treated differently by FEMA and under the 'Stafford Act; and (3) the need for FEMA to re-examine its criteria for evaluating disaster declarations for rural tribal communities.

Background on the Colville Tribes and Major Disasters on the Colville Reservation

Although now considered a single Indian tribe, the Confederated Tribes of the Colville Reservation is a confederation of twelve aboriginal tribes and bands from across eastern Washington State. The present-day Colville Reservation is in north-central Washington State and was established by Executive Order in 1872. The Colville Reservation covers approximately 1.4 million acres and its boundaries include parts of Okanogan and Ferry counties. The CCT has more than 9,400 enrolled members, making it one of the largest Indian tribes in the Pacific Northwest, and the second largest in the State of Washington. About half of the CCT's members live on or near the Colville Reservation. Of the 1.4 million acres that comprise the Colville Reservation, 922,240 acres are forested land, and 660,000 of the forested acres are commercial timber land.

The Colville Tribes has endured three major disasters during the past five years. The first occurred in July 2012, when a major wind storm and flash flood toppled trees, destroyed power lines and tribal infrastructure, and blocked or damaged roads over an area of several hundred thousand acres. Although damage occurred reservation-wide, the community of Keller was most heavily affected by the storm. Homes were lost or damaged, and residents with undamaged homes were left without power for extended periods. The community water infrastructure was damaged by uprooted trees, and rural residents outside of the Keller community were without power for even longer. The Keller disaster occurred before the tribal amendments to the Stafford Act became law and the CCT worked with the State of Washington to ensure that the state included damage to the Colville Reservation as part of its request for a Presidential Disaster Declaration (PDD). President Obama issued the

PDD, which enabled the Colville Tribes and other affected jurisdictions to obtain assistance through FEMA's Public Assistance program.

Two years later, in 2014, four fires, collectively referred to as the "Carlton Complex" fires, burned 256,108 acres in communities near the Colville Reservation. While the Colville Reservation damage was comparatively small and limited to uninhabited rangeland, CCT personnel assisted local governments in the suppression and recovery efforts. The Carlton Complex fire burned more than 300 homes and other structures and affected life and property throughout two watersheds.

Most recently, in 2015, the Colville Tribes endured the most destructive fire on an Indian reservation in recorded history. The North Star and Okanogan Complex fires collectively burned more than 255,000 acres on the Colville Reservation—nearly 20 percent of the total land base. Approximately one-fourth of the commercial timber land on the Reservation burned or was affected, which included 788 million board feet of timber. These two fires were part of the worst wildfire season in Washington state history that saw more than 121 fires ignited during a four-day period from August 10–14, 2015.

The 2015 fires statewide resulted in the deaths of three firefighters, a non-firefighting fatality, 21 injuries, and ultimately burned more than 1 million acres. The Okanogan Complex fire surpassed the 2014 Carlton Complex fire as the largest fire in Washington state history. 2015 marked the first year ever that Washington state officials asked residents to volunteer to assist in fighting wildfires.

For both the 2014 Carlton Complex and the 2015 fires, Washington State Governor Inslee requested, and President Obama issued, PDDs that authorized Public Assistance for both the Colville Tribes and the affected local governments. In both cases, however, FEMA denied the Governor's requests for assistance for homeowners under FEMA's Individual Assistance program. Following FEMA's denial of the Governor's Individual Assistance request for the 2015 fires, the Colville Tribes submitted its own separate request for Individual Assistance for on-reservation residents. FEMA denied that request as well.

Catastrophic Wildfires Should be Treated Differently by FEMA and in the Stafford Act

Currently, neither FEMA nor the Stafford Act adequately addresses the full extent of damage caused by massive, catastrophic wildfires. While FEMA did establish an "Erosion Threat Assessment Reduction Team" to assess post-fire rehabilitation needs, the funding for carrying out most of those activities must be secured from other sources. Funding for immediate landscape stabilization can be charged to the Department of the Interior's Wildland Fire Management program, but longer term Burn Area Rehabilitation funding is extremely limited for Indian tribes nationwide, as are funds for replanting.

In the next few years, the single biggest task will be replanting trees burned during the 2015 wildfire season. Although the Colville Tribes has and continues to seek alternative funding sources, the only dedicated federal source of replanting funds for Indian forests are BIA forestry funds. The BIA has a statutory obligation to replant Indian forest land but its average annual reforestation budget is approximately $3.2 million for tribes nationwide.

The BIA's entire $3.2 million budget would cover planting of less than 11,000 acres. Relying only on BIA funds would mean the hundreds of thousands of acres of forest land on the Colville Reservation may not be replanted for decades, if ever. In contrast to the obstacles the CCT must endure given the limitations of the BIA's reforestation budget, the U.S. Forest Service is already implementing its plans to replant the 9,095 acres of national forest land affected by the 2014 and 2015 fires.

The CCT has traditionally relied on forest products and stumpage as primary sources of revenue to fund tribal government programs. The long-term damage to the CCT's economy and government will be felt for decades unless replanting can take place soon. The loss of forest lands will also have a lasting cultural impact on the Colville Tribes and its members. The fires devastated big game populations, cultural plants, and culturally significant sites reservation-wide.

FEMA programs do not address the full extent of the damage caused by catastrophic fire events, including fires on non-Indian federal lands. FEMA should provide immediate assistance for fire suppression, stabilization, and landscape rehabilitation. For Indian forest land, FEMA should also provide assistance for replanting in light of the United States' statutory obligations to reforest Indian forest land.

One approach would be to create a separate disaster declaration category for catastrophic fire events, like what was included in Title IX of the House-passed Resilient Federal Forests Act of 2015 (H.R. 2647). That provision would have authorized the President to declare a major disaster for wildfires on federal lands (including Indian trust lands) and authorized FEMA to aid the Departments of the Interior and Agriculture for extraordinary wildfire suppression costs that exceed the 10-year average. The scope and severity of fire events continues to grow and this type of solution is needed to ensure that both Indian and non-Indian communities can fully recover from massive fire events.

FEMA Should Re-examine its Criteria to Ensure Rural Tribal Communities are Treated Fairly

One of FEMA's criteria for evaluating requests for Individual Assistance is concentrations of damages. As stated in FEMA regulations, "High concentrations of damages generally indicate a greater need for Federal assistance than widespread and scattered damages throughout a State." 44 C.F.R. § 206.48(b)(1). The FEMA pilot guidance for tribal disaster declarations did not modify this criterion or otherwise change how FEMA applies it to tribes.

FEMA has never publicly articulated the basis for its denials of the Washington state and Colville Tribes' requests for Individual Assistance for the 2014 and 2015 fires. Based on discussions with local officials and our congressional delegation, however, we believe that the fact that much of the damage was widespread over a large geographic area was the primary reason for FEMA's denials.

Rural areas like the Colville Reservation are inherently prone to a lower concentration of damages based on population density. However, the economic, social, agricultural, and cultural damages from major disasters often impact rural communities much more severely than in metropolitan areas. This was the case with the affected residents of the Colville Reservation, many of whom lost access to health care and other essentials due to extended road closures. Other tribal members lost their livelihoods when cattle and rangeland burned, which are damages that have persisted and will continue long after the fires were extinguished.

In the 114th Congress, members of the Washington state congressional delegation introduced the "Individual Assistance Improvement Act of 2015" (H.R. 4243), which would have waived the concentration of damages criterion for rural communities in certain instances. Until a permanent legislative or administrative fix can be made, FEMA should amend existing guidance or issue new guidance that makes clear that rural Indian tribes will not be denied assistance based on concentration of damages.

The CHAIRMAN. Thank you, Director Desautel.

With that, we will turn to questions. The Chairman and Vice Chairman will save their questions until the end, at least for this hearing. That could change from hearing to hearing. That is how we will start. We will start with Senator Lankford.

STATEMENT OF HON. JAMES LANKFORD, U.S. SENATOR FROM OKLAHOMA

Senator LANKFORD. Thank you very much.

I appreciate all of you being here and appreciate your testimony and the conversation on this. This is a pilot program that has very far reaching implications. As this dais has heard me say before, Oklahoma is a little different in the way we handle reservation and non-reservation areas.

As a non-reservation State, there is a tremendous amount of area that is historic tribal area where there are no businesses in trust or lands in trust or tribal headquarters that are there. My question really relates to this program and how this would work and function.

It is my understanding that for a tribe to make a disaster declaration, it is $250,000 worth of damage. For a State to make a declaration, it is $1 million. Is that correct?

Mr. AMPARO. Senator, you are referring to what is termed as a "minimum damage amount." For States, it is a $1 million damage amount. For tribes, it is $250,000 but that is not a threshold as if you have $250,000, there is a guarantee for a declaration.

In the pilot, this is part of the comments we have received in our listening sessions, the $1 million for tribes was just too high.

Senator LANKFORD. So how do you deal with areas of overlap? For instance, we have many communities where we may have a city and county that would have issues; you would also have tribal areas within that same historic area. What accounts for overlap in an area like Oklahoma where we are a non-reservation location?

Mr. AMPARO. There is coordination with Albert Ashwood, the State Director of Emergency Management in Oklahoma, close coordination with our regional office, Region 6 out of Denton, Texas, with the tribes and the State, the tribes and the State being the eligible entities to be grantees.

There are situations where we have seen even tribes that did not have land but had infrastructure that was damaged that worked closely with the State on a declaration request. I would tell you the way that overlap is adjudicated is through coordination between the State and our regional office.

Senator LANKFORD. Let me ask about the pilot, the functioning of it.

We are approaching the end of it in many ways as we look on the horizon at 2020. Is that the end of the pilot program?

Mr. AMPARO. We do not have an official end to the pilot program. It has taken us several years of consultation with tribes to develop the pilot guidance. It is now in effect. It will be in effect for at least two years at which time we would evaluate through data collection what our findings are and what future changes we would make to guidance.

Senator LANKFORD. What metrics are you using at this point to be able to determine that? As you say you are putting it out to them; you have two years to evaluate it. Do you already have those metrics in place to see what you want to try to achieve?

Mr. AMPARO. I think Senator Murkowski mentioned a couple of the issues we have with the two declarations requests that came through. There were different types of events. They were unique in the way they are.

We continue to hear comments from Indian country on things that may not have been contemplated where we have put the guidance out. We are open to those in this pilot period to account for them.

I think just a sheer number of how many declarations were granted versus ones that were not, it is not our measure. We would like to be able to is compare a period of time under this pilot guidance to a period of time that we were not under this pilot guidance and look to see what the findings are and be open to what the data tells us.

Senator LANKFORD. Mr. President?

Mr. BEGAYE. Thank you, Senator.

We are asking this Committee to make that disaster balance a permanent designation of $250,000 because it really is difficult for communities and rural areas to reach that $1 million threshold that we had to abide by earlier.

Now with this new guidance, we are asking the Committee to keep that at $250,000 as the amendment for damages.

Senator LANKFORD. Let me ask a question as well. Is there any properties, locations or structures that are excluded from a disaster declaration? If a tribe says these are sacred lands and here is a certain building, there is a house of worship, or there is a meeting place or a business, is there any type of structure that FEMA would say we do not recognize and will not allot funds to that?

Mr. AMPARO. No, sir. Quite the contrary, we work very closely with the tribes. We have environmental and historic preservation experts. We also look to the tribes to provide us some of the cultural experts on tribal lands.

In the declarations we have worked specifically with the Oglala Sioux Tribe in a large disaster, our reliance on tribal expertise is immense. That is the direction in which we are moving.

Senator LANKFORD. Just clarification, sacred lands, houses of worship, meeting spots, all of those would be included?

Mr. AMPARO. Yes, sir, as tribal infrastructure.

Senator LANKFORD. Thank you.

The CHAIRMAN. Senator Cortez Masto.

STATEMENT OF HON. CATHERINE CORTEZ MASTO, U.S. SENATOR FROM NEVADA

Senator CORTEZ MASTO. Thank you, Mr. Chair.

Mr. Amparo and Mr. Booth, thank you very much. Thank you all for joining us. I have a specific question that impacts my State of Nevada.

Most people do not realize there are actually 32 Indian reservations and colonies that stretch across Nevada. Unfortunately, in January of this year, we had a severe flooding event in northern Nevada that impacted the Pyramid Lake Paiute Tribe.

I have similar questions when it comes to the emergency declaration because I know under the Pilot Guidance you just released, there is a requirement that the emergency declaration can be made by the chief executive of the affected tribal government or governor of the State but it has to be made within 30 days of the occurrence of the incident.

In my State, if the Pyramid Lake Paiute Tribe decides to work with the governor, who has not declared that emergency yet because they are still assessing the damage, can you address for me whether that 30 days is going to impact whether they are able to receive the funds or not or how you handle that 30 day timeline? Mr. AMPARO. Senator, the 30 day is a regulatory timeframe that we have.

We are aware of the preliminary damage assessments that are underway along with the work the tribe and the State are working together on. Our commitment is to continue to work closely.

The impetus behind the Tribal Declaration Guidance and the change to the Stafford Act through the Senate Recovery Act was to provide an option to the tribe, an option that they can go with a declaration in partnership with the State and that has occurred and continues to occur throughout the country.

Quite frankly, that is a great partnership between tribes and States or tribes have gone directly to the President through this. That provides their option. That option still exists but our commitment is to work closely with the State and the tribe.

Senator CORTEZ MASTO. Just for clarification, if they do not get it within that 30 days, you are still willing to accept that declaration and work with them to respond and provide the appropriate monetary response if possible?

Mr. AMPARO. That is correct. I would say that the State and the tribe can request an extension prior to the end of the 30 days.

Senator CORTEZ MASTO. Okay. That could be normal course?

Mr. AMPARO. Yes, ma'am.

Senator CORTEZ MASTO. Maybe this is something you can provide to me later. I would like to know how active the regional tribal liaison is for region 9, particularly leading up to the severe event. If you could provide that to me in writing after this that would be fantastic.

Mr. AMPARO. I absolutely will, Senator. I would also take the time to say that among tribes, your State is among the greatest number participating in the flood insurance program as well. That is a good thing.

Senator CORTEZ MASTO. You just dovetailed right into the next discussion. As we all know, the reauthorization of the National Flood Insurance Program is very important. We also know that participation in the program overall is low among Native American communities.

Can you talk a little bit about what effort FEMA has undertaken to boost participation in this program and ensure that these communities have affordable flood insurance?

Mr. AMPARO. Senator, I would like to be able to get back to you with more specifics but I will tell you what I do know.

One, we announced yesterday consultation that will begin with Indian country on hazard mitigation planning review. That is an effort that we are undergoing to ensure that tribes have hazard mitigation plans in place prior to events from happening.

In the same sense, part of my opening oral testimony has been to show you a bit about how agency has evolved as well. Working directly with tribes has increased our capacity internally.

I believe in Region IX, your region, there is more than one regional tribal liaison. Now we are including in their body of work the responsibility to talk about all FEMA programs as we have interaction in both consultation but also in participation at one of our training institutes or outreach that we do to the tribes.

We are providing information about the National Flood Insurance Program and what steps tribes can take to be active participants.

Senator CORTEZ MASTO. Thank you very much.

Mr. AMPARO. Thank you, Senator.

The CHAIRMAN. Senator Murkowski.

Senator MURKOWSKI. Thank you, Mr. Chairman.

I want to give a special shout out to Mr. Booth, who I understand hails originally from Metlakatla.

Mr. BOOTH. That is correct, Senator.

Senator MURKOWSKI. It is good to have you here. We appreciate your leadership.

I mentioned in my opening comments the request from two villages. The Village of Nutok on December 24 applied for a presidential declaration of major disaster. They had destruction of their barge landing, sewage disposal systems, solid waste site, boat dock,

45 homes damaged and were concerned they will lose their water supply later this year.

Again, the response to Nutok was that this request was denied because it did not fit the requirements of the Stafford Act. We recognize that Nutok's request was unique. This slow moving disaster, as I mentioned, is unique to FEMA.

Even more recent was Kivalina's request. They submitted their application for major disaster declaration on January 15, 2017. It was denied on February 1. In that application for disaster, they cited severe storms, flooding, persistent erosion, storm led to shutdown of the airport and does not allow for opportunities for evacuations.

Clearly, these are situations that anyone would look at and say, this is a disaster area. If it is not a disaster immediately, it is clearly a disaster in the making.

The question I have today is they were not given a reason for the denial except that based on FEMA's review of the major disaster declaration, it was not appropriate to address the situation in these communities.

It kind of begs the question what is appropriate? What is FEMA's path forward for communities whether it is Nutok or Kivalina today, Shishmaref or other communities tomorrow? If you can provide any information or any reasoning behind the denials to me and whether or not FEMA was able to offer anything else in terms of guidance or assistance?

I am trying to understand whether there are written policies out there that guide FEMA with these slow moving disasters and where are we with situations as these communities are facing?

Mr. AMPARO. Senator Murkowski, I will tell you that I agree with you. The situation of a slow moving disaster in the making is something not contemplated under the Stafford Act but it is a situation that we face, I think collectively "we."

In that vein, I will also say that situations like this would call for more than a single-pronged approach in terms of FEMA or Federal declaration and one that is more akin to a whole of government approach.

We do have a hazard mitigation grant program to allow for taking efforts prior to a disaster to lessen the impacts of a disaster, yet even within that program, I think that would not solve the problem faced by the communities.

Senator MURKOWSKI. Let me ask you then, because I agree with everything that you have said. One of the reasons that these applications were submitted, was recognized by the communities that these were unique, was because they have tried and have come looking for direct appropriations, an earmark.

They have contacted the Corps trying to work through the Army Corps of Engineers and have basically been told, well, until you fall off the edge, there is no relief for you.

When the Obama Administration announced its climate resilience grants last year, they thought ah ha, this is exactly where we can go and they made application through the Administration. Alaska villages got nothing from that.

They said okay, you have the Stafford Act out there and if not there, where? Is this something that you will commit to me and to our Alaska Native villages, not just the Alaska Native villages, but we have other communities as well that are in jeopardy, that we can be working through to define how we can address some of these threats before we see that loss of life, before we see an entire village wiped out?

Mr. AMPARO. Senator, you have my commitment that I will work with you, your staff, and the Alaska Native villages on this issue, including bringing in other Federal agency partners that may be necessary.

Senator MURKOWSKI. You are right. It does need to be a whole of agency approach. Again, we are looking for guidance and somebody to step up and take point because to this point in time, no agency has been willing to shoulder it.

It is a significant task but it is one that I think we recognize we have to address. We are going to have to address more situations like this rather than less going forward.

Thank you, Mr. Chairman.

The CHAIRMAN. Thank you, Senator Murkowski.

Senator Cantwell.

Senator CANTWELL. Thank you, Mr. Chairman.

I would like to turn to Mr. Desautel's comments as it relates to the impacts that rural communities are seeing and FEMA's designation. Mr. Desautel mentioned how two requests by rural communities in our State were turned down by FEMA frankly because the way the definition works, it does not recognize rural communities.

I do not know, Mr. Amparo, if you have any comments about that definition and how it came into place. Just so my colleagues know, this would be like saying Galena, Taos, Aspen or something does not have an impact because there is not a concentration when in reality, the impact to that community is just as devastating.

The fact that it is a rural community, maybe based on tourism, maybe in our case, at least in Twisp and other aspects of the Carlton Complex fire, the workforce was basically unable to locate in the region.

They continued to support the hotel and continued to support all this but because your definition says it has to have this concentration of population and this much assessment of housing damage across the population area, these communities do not get any help.

Mr. AMPARO. My comments in this area would be that I do not believe it is the definition of a concentration of damage or is it an issue of rural vs. urban. It is more of what the aggregate damage and destruction was.

The Stafford Act is for supplementary assistance when an event has exceeded the capacity of the tribe or the State. In the case of Colville, I do not have the damage assessments in front of me, I believe it was more the case of the damages in aggregate, not the fact that the damages occurred in an area that was rural.

Senator CANTWELL. I am pretty sure they were pretty significant if he said there was 20 percent loss in revenue. Mr. Desautel, do you want to address that?

Mr. DESAUTEL. We never really got a response as to why we were denied but that was our assumption. From a damages standpoint, we still do not know to this day. We have been working on getting a full assessment for a year and a half but the damage was so vast, we still do not have a good handle on what that number might be as far as total economic loss or total resource damage.

Senator CANTWELL. Is it in the hundreds of millions?

Mr. DESAUTEL. I would guess it is north of $100 million. It is $100 million just in timber revenue.

Senator CANTWELL. Okay, so pretty significant damage when that is your operating revenue for your government?

Mr. DESAUTEL. Yes, ma'am.

Senator CANTWELL. Pretty significant.

I think, Mr. Amparo, I really do believe this Committee has to come back and address this or other committees because I think we are going to continue to see this kind of devastation. I do not think these trends are going to stop, whether it is flooding or fire. They are not going to stop.

I think the point is that while you are thinking of it as the impact of damage, you have to think of it as a percentage of that rural economy. What happens in the State of Washington, a rural economy that exists on a major thoroughfare, is the anchor for the entire region is decimated and people cannot go to work because there is no housing. It becomes a problem.

I wanted to touch, Mr. Desautel, on another related issue particularly since my colleague from Alaska is here and she and I have worked so hard on trying to get out a timber bill.

One of the things I believe you have been able to do successfully on the Colville Reservation is the type of fuel reduction that has helped in protecting some of your timberlands by creating barriers and efforts to better manage the forest, is that correct?

Mr. DESAUTEL. That is correct. We have done active forest management which was commercial type treatments that has reduced stocking and changed species composition for those acres so those acres are more resilient to fire.

We have done other fuels type treatment, especially in those areas where we see risk to communities. We also see resources pulled when we have active fires.

Senator CANTWELL. Even though we saw devastating seasons, you saw success in having done that kind of work. If we could do more of it in the future, it would be helpful to protecting our communities?

Mr. DESAUTEL. Yes, I think you are exactly right. We have done a lot of it. We have not done enough of it. It is definitely a pace and scale thing that there are lots of acres that are growing into fire regime twos and threes, for those familiar with that, where they are very susceptible to insect, disease and fire.

You need to make sure we are treating enough that we are keeping pace with that while making progress towards making those acres resilient for future fires and disturbance.

Senator CANTWELL. Thank you.

Thank you, Mr. Chairman.

The CHAIRMAN. Senator Franken.

Senator FRANKEN. Thank you, Mr. Chairman. Again, congratulations on heading up this Committee.

As I mentioned in my opening statement, I am concerned about the Prairie Island Indian Community in my State. Prairie Island

Indian Community is located essentially on an island in the Mississippi River on the river's floodplain.

The nuclear reactor and the nuclear waste sites are located about 600 yards from the nearest home on Prairie Island. The community is obviously concerned about the potential for emergency situations causes by either the power plant or by the flooding. This concern is exacerbated because there are few evacuation routes off the reservation.

My question for both Mr. Amparo and Mr. Booth is basically, has FEMA consulted with the Prairie Island Reservation to develop an emergency preparedness plan?

Mr. AMPARO. Senator Franken, I spoke earlier with our regional office out of Chicago, Region V. I have information that they have a very good relationship with the Prairie Island Community, specifically because of their proximity to the nuclear plant.

Because of that, tribal government staff has hosted and participated in several of the FEMA tribal emergency training. Additionally, the community has participated in exercises that have been offered by our regional office as well.

There are requirements as well from the nuclear power plant site to help host those types of exercises to ensure that the community is aware of hazards, evacuation planning and the like.

Senator FRANKEN. So there are evacuation routes in place and a plan in place in case of an event?

Mr. AMPARO. Yes, sir. I can get back to you with specifics on that plan and those evacuation routes. I do know having spoken with our regional office that there is a good working relationship with the community.

Senator FRANKEN. Thank you.

Obviously every tribe is unique and so is its relationship with the State government. In Minnesota, tribes and State government have a good working relationship when it comes to preparedness and relief from disasters.

It is my understanding that the Tribal Stafford Act does not outline ways for the States to work collaboratively with tribes and obviously coordination between tribal and State governments is very important during disaster relief efforts and during the events.

Can you speak, Mr. Amparo or Mr. Booth, to what FEMA does to foster the relationship between the States and the tribes?

Mr. AMPARO. Yes, sir. I outlined a bit of what we went into just with the consultation for our Tribal Declaration Guidance in working with tribes. Prior to coming to work at FEMA, I worked with the State of Florida in emergency management. We worked with our Miccosukee and Seminole Indian tribes there.

It is a relationship which we value because many times there are declarations or there are disasters that are not declared. I think we have spoken about several here today. The relationship between a State and the tribes pays dividends in helping disaster survivors where they are.

We have hosted training sessions. The exercises that we do are both with tribes and with State partners, again valuing that. Last year, when we did the Cascadia exercise, the Cascadia subduction zone, we had 24 tribes participate along with three States, so they were working jointly at the State level and also at the local emergency management level.

Senator FRANKEN. I was wondering also about the counties. Obviously that coordination seems to be key to me because it is all hands on deck during an emergency.

Mr. AMPARO. Locally is where the resources come first as well, whether it is a fire engine.

Senator FRANKEN. Or getting electricity back up.

Mr. AMPARO. That is right, so it is the Rural Electric Cooperative that is providing services.

Senator FRANKEN. Thank you, gentlemen.

Thank you, Mr. Chairman.

The CHAIRMAN. This question is for either Mr. Amparo or Mr. Booth.

President Begaye talked about when they had the mine disaster and the spill on the reservation that essentially FEMA took the position that all the other agencies were in there taking care of things.

You talked about working with other agencies. Tell us how you work with those other agencies and when other agencies are involved, how do you make that decision to come in or not come? I want you to specifically respond to the situation Mr. Begaye described.

In other words, there is a big difference between you coming in immediately and providing disaster assistance and relief assistance or taking the position, well, there are other agencies taking care of that, so we are not going to.

I want you to respond to that and then I am going to ask President Begaye to kind of tell me what he thinks of that, how it works and how it should work. I will start with you.

Mr. AMPARO. Sir, I am a Federal public servant and I am an emergency manager. When faced with situations like this, we certainly recognize where FEMA has authority to operate. Sometimes our assistance is not the emergency assistance, it is reimbursement assistance. It is dollars to help pay for what other agencies can provide.

I certainly know that in the spill, the Environmental Protection Agency had jurisdiction but we do work as a interagency. I think that is what is expected of us as Federal servants. We work through what is known as the Emergency Support Function Leadership Group, the ESFLG, where we have all interagency partners there. We discuss the threats out there.

It is also my understanding that in that spill, the Environmental Protection Agency set up a Unified Coordination Group. I can go back and get much more specifics and respond to you with much more clarity but I will tell you, at least from the posture of our agency, our agency's leadership, we do see ourselves as a coordinating entity, even in ensuring that the right agencies get to be able to support the communities and individuals impacted by disaster.

The CHAIRMAN. President Begaye, would you discuss how that worked on the ground and how you think it should work or could be improved?

Mr. BEGAYE. Yes. The response we got from FEMA, this is what they said, "The vast majority of the response and recovery efforts for this event, Gold King Mine spill, fall under the authorities of other Federal agencies," which meant to us the U.S. EPA.

I met with USDA and asked them, why aren't you helping us? They said, "We were told that we are not the lead agency; that EPA is the lead agency and we are not to assist unless they ask us to come to the table."

I said, well, why can't you just use your normal, regular responsibilities and help us clean out the ditches where the spill came in and just help us from that standpoint because we are talking about farmers and so forth? Why can't you just come under your own program, not under EPA?

We understand this whole dynamic that has taken place as far as EPA saying back off other Federal agencies; we are the lead in this disaster and we will ask you when we need you to come to assist Navajo Nation.

We are asking that this policy change, that there be a definite "collaboration among Federal agencies when any disaster occurs." FEMA, HHS, or any Federal agency should come to assist in any type of major disaster, declaration or emergency declaration.

I believe that needs to be clarified also because there is one category for major disaster declaration and then there is another category for emergency declaration. Under the major disaster, they will come and help assist farmers, ranchers with livestock and crop losses. Under emergency declaration, we understand they could not help in that instance.

All of those need to be clarified. All Federal agencies need to be called on to assist in any disaster, especially in the magnitude of the Gold King Mine.

The CHAIRMAN. Now I am going to go to Governor Chavarria and ask essentially the same question on the Pilot Guidance, if it is what it should be or if it should be modified. If so, how?

Before I do, did you have any response, Mr. Amparo?

In regard to President Begaye?

I am very concerned. When a tribe or anyone else has to start trying to figure out which agency is going to help and each agency says, it is really that agency, it can be a very frustrating and difficult situation. Particularly in an emergency response, I am concerned about that.

Mr. AMPARO. Senator, I have a response and I will tell you that I do have questions. I believe there is an exigency that a tribe must have the right answers when faced with a disaster. I agree with that.

I also believe that, quite frankly, one of the things we are doing with our outreach, with our tribal liaisons, is to talk about what FEMA programs do and do not do, and what other Federal agencies can provide so that it is not when the disaster is at our doorstep that we are having that conversation. We can preplan and know ahead of time.

There is more work. Part of my statement is to say that there is much more work for us to do, including our other Federal agency partners, to work with Indian country about what our programs provide and how we can synchronize them so that they are efficient.

The CHAIRMAN. President Begaye.

Mr. BEGAYE. Just the word jurisdiction really implies that this is our responsibility. It is our jurisdiction and not yours. That language needs to be taken out.

The other thing is right answers. To me, it should not be that. If you provide the right answers, we will help you. That should not be the response of FEMA. They should be coming alongside and helping us develop those applications because we do not know what the right answers are or what the right languages are.

We need FEMA to come alongside and help us help those people who are losing homes, vehicles, farms, crops, irrigation and things like that. We need them to come alongside us and treat us as human beings.

The CHAIRMAN. I think that is the key. Even if it is not a FEMA response, it is a FEMA responsibility to make sure that the agency, whoever is the responder, is taking care of things. That should be a FEMA role as well as direct response if you are not the direct responder. That is kind of what I am getting at here.

Governor Chavarria, your thoughts?

Mr. CHAVARRIA. I also feel that it is open to interpretation. Yes, we have the Pilot Guidance document but it comes with challenges. It is a new process for both the tribes and FEMA. We are the first tribe in Region 6 to utilize the Stafford Act amendments to allow the tribes to go direct.

However, as the changes to the Stafford Act allows tribes to see that direct disaster declaration are promulgated, FEMA may be better served by implanting a training program that better communicates the regulatory requirements associated with being a direct guarantee.

This would better enable the tribes to make an informed decision regarding FEMA's assistance may it be for your public assistance or your individual assistance. Those are different categories that fall within FEMA.

It is very important. It is not a catchall because FEMA is not the answer to all the disasters. You have the Corps, BIA, the Bureau of Reclamation, the Forest Service, and the Park Service. All these other agencies are out there but how do they fit in because the time of need is where that dollar needs to hit our communities.

We have had bad experiences as sub-grantees. Our first disaster happened on August 21, 2011. We did not get the funds until almost a year later. By then, you have additional events. That is very important. Yes, there is a process. However, what is critical that starts off anything is your hazard mitigation plan. If you do not have a hazard mitigation plan, you do not even qualify. That is important.

As the President said, the facts need to be addressed to all tribes and have a good understanding of the regulatory requirements because even though you do not meet that $250,000 threshold, you are not even eligible for financial assistance. That is hurtful and again, it is not a catchall.

The best way that FEMA and tribes can really get together is sit down, have a training session, so both sides understand what the roles and responsibilities are or what we are accountable for on both sides of aisle.

The CHAIRMAN. Exactly right. We are on the front end of this, so it is building the process and making sure it works and fostering understanding.

Mr. CHAVARRIA. Yes.

The CHAIRMAN. Director Desautel, anything else along that line from your recent experience?

Mr. DESAUTEL. One thing I think FEMA struggles with is in our area, when there were disaster declarations, they used the county records to assess value to try to get to that threshold but for trust properties, they are not assessed by the county so they do not have a good way to value resources whether it be homes or land damage.

I think that is also something that needs to be assessed to determine what values are placed on tribal lands. If you do not have an accounting system like the counties have to document what the value is, it is really difficult for us to manage the process and show $250,000 worth of damages.

The CHAIRMAN. Mr. Amparo, anything that you want to add to respond to that?

Mr. AMPARO. Yes. I think that is a great point. It is one we heard very loud and clear. In our Tribal Declarations Guidance, we took that into account. Now we will go to the tribe and ask them to provide us that information.

There has also been some great movement with the Oglala Sioux Tribe where they are working to get better numbers themselves. When we are active in a joint field office, we work with the tribe to help them either map the roads or help them get more but I would like to have our tribal advisor talk a little bit to the Governor's comments and our efforts to better create an environment where we are sharing more information.

Mr. BOOTH. Thank you, Mr. Amparo.

Mr. Chairman and Mr. Vice Chairman, to address the Governor's comments about training and integration with our rollout plan that we started last week, we started off with a national webinar/conference call.

It continued this week at the United South and Eastern Tribes where we had our Tribal Consultation Coordinator for the Tribal Declarations Pilot Guidance give that presentation so we can collect those comments and get the word out.

We are going to continue doing this as immediately as next week at the National Congress of American Indians' Executive Winter Session and will continue as we move forward both at regional and national tribal associations.

The CHAIRMAN. I think it is very important. Again, you are on the front end of the process. You need to create that understanding, get the good input and build the best approach you can with all the tribes.

I apologize, Vice Chairman, for going over my time. I should have broken that up into two but I did not realize that some of my questions would go as long as they did. However, you go ahead and complete with any questions that you have.

Senator UDALL. That is the Chairman's discretion. No problem there. It is good to finish your train of thought and get the points in. We really appreciate that.

What the Chairman has outlined here is very helpful. His approach and my approach I think will be very similar in terms of trying to get to the situation where we get help in these disasters.

Both tribal leaders have shown they want to do, Mr. Amparo, everything they can on the ground at the time of a tribal emergency to try to help their people. If there are situations where, for example in the Gold King Mine spill, the Navajo Nation had specific expenses they were expending as a part of this emergency. They wanted to have a relationship with the Federal agency to figure out whether or not they were going to be reimbursed, how they were going to be reimbursed, and what the timetable was going to be.

Following up on some of what Chairman Hoeven said, it seems to me one of the issues here is the issue if EPA is supposed to be the lead, is EPA, in your opinion, capable of being lead in a disaster? I thought FEMA was the disaster agency.

How does that happen all of a sudden with an agency like the EPA, because they happened to be the agency that caused the problem? As President Begaye said, here you had a mine that backed up, filled water and filled water and filled water and the EPA contractor punctured a hole in it and that caused the flood.

That is what caused the flood and now they are in charge of the emergency. How does that happen? I am wondering do you assess or look at this and say, well, they know all about floods and disas- ters with mines and are capable of doing this? How do they get to be the lead?

It seemed to me you are the lead in a way on a disaster. Let me tell you that when you have come into New Mexico, we have had disasters on reservation and off reservation. I have seen some very impressive work by FEMA. We had the Cerro Grande Fire in Los Alamos which wiped out 400 homes. FEMA was in there and you did some incredible work.

Part of asking this question is trying to get to the heart of how do we get the very best response for Native communities when it comes to these disasters like both Governors have described?

Mr. Amparo, can you answer that briefly because I do not want to go much over what the Chairman went. I know we are both busy here today.

Mr. AMPARO. First, to the President, let me first say that there is no secret code in terms of asking the right questions. Our commitment from our regional office is to have our experts work with tribes on requests they make of us to ensure that we are reviewing documents for them prior to their submission. That is something we do.

Second, to commend Governor Chavarria for speaking about a mitigation plan and talking about that being the start and where we need to go, that is an area that is refreshing for us because we know that understanding what vulnerabilities and risks are prior to event changes the outcome.

Our commitment is to work with other Federal agencies, ultimately to support the tribe. We are going to continue to do that.

The Chairman mentioned that and I have questions. I will have to look more at it with our regional office but our commitment will be to work closely with the tribes and should an incident like this happen again, ensure that the outcomes are the ones that are expected.

Senator UDALL. Thank you very much for that.

President Begaye, I know you are an incredible champion for the Navajo people in terms of trying to deal with this disaster. You were everyplace. I believe you and some of your officials went to water tanks which were going to be provided for drinking water and it ended up that some of that was tainted with oil. You said, these cannot be for drinking water.

I know how upset you are and you stated very well what happened. The new Guidance that has come out from FEMA, in your opinion, are we headed in the right direction on that?

Mr. BEGAYE. Consultation is always a thing that we have to do. Having an advisory council is always the right thing to have. Having the right benchmarks, $250,000 against $1 million, is the right thing to do. Those are good starting points.

The webinar, they are always helpful if we can have access to Internet. That is always a challenge for us, especially on Navajo when 30 percent of our people have access and 70 percent do not. We have those challenges.

However, the new principle that they put in place, we made comments on it. We believe the consultation is really important. It is helping to clarify some of these terms I mentioned earlier, "major disaster declaration" versus "emergency declaration," our actual liability partner or potential liability partner, what does that terminology mean, what are they?

If we can answer those types of questions, we can better answer, especially when we apply for disaster assistance and we know what language to use, how to approach FEMA and other Federal agencies. I endorse that. I feel that is something we need.

Having a tribal liaison person, of course, is always very helpful. Having a FEMA office on Navajo would be tremendously helpful. We are as big as West Virginia and we should have our own FEMA office located on Navajo Nation. That is how we can really resolve these issues.

Senator UDALL. Thank you.

President Begaye, for you and I, I think one of the frustrating things in this particular situation with EPA was that the EPA Administrator came out from the beginning. Now I am talking about the injury to the farmers that happened on the land. We have been to many of the same farms. She said from the beginning, "We take responsibility. We are going to take responsibility. We are going to make sure those farmers get paid for their damages."

That is the way we proceeded but there was a little glitch. Over here there was a little independent agency within EPA that has to make a decision on liability. About a year later, they tell us, sorry, you have to file a lawsuit and go to court. We were on one track and now we are on another track.

You and I are working on legislation with your Washington office and with others. I would just ask you to urge the Committee, this

is your opportunity to tell the Committee why these folks should
be compensated.

You described what happened and how the Navajo people live an
agricultural life and what they are doing out there and you would
urge us because we need to pass legislation to help these farmers.
This is really important.

This is your opportunity to speak to the Committee as a whole.
There are only two of us here but believe me, everyone else will
hear it.

Mr. BEGAYE. Thank you, Senator.

When a Federal agency says we caused a spill, we will hold ourselves responsible and we will make sure that all the impacted people will be compensated, when that statement comes out of the
mouth of a Federal agency, we expect that to happen.

Just within the last few weeks, I got a letter that says we will
not give you a dime. We will not help you because there is this
Federal sovereignty that exists meaning that we cannot be sued,
we cannot help you.

None of our farmers have ever been helped. This is when a Federal agency says, we will hold ourselves responsible. When that
statement is made, we expect and I believe this Committee will
have to hold that agency's feet to the fire to say you said that, it
came out of your mouth in a Senate hearing, then you ought to pay
up.

These farmers are hurting. Not a single farmer has been compensated. That to me is criminal. That should never happen within
the trust responsibility, trust relationship that we have, government-to-government relationship we have.

Every one of those farmers today are still hurting, over a year
and a half. None of them have been compensated. They are still out
there. You and I visited, we have been out to the farms. They weep;
they are crying, so the disaster is continuing.

Farming is not just one crop. It is multiple crops, multiple seasons. When you cut off the water stream, when you are not able
to use the water, we are talking about a disaster that lasts for two
to three years. That is happening to our farmers today.

I am asking this Committee to hold EPA's word and let them
compensate every one of our farmers that has been hurt. That is
our priority.

Of course we also, as tribal nations, need to be compensated for
the work we have put in too because they said they did it and they
would hold themselves responsible. To this day, they have not.
That letter specially says, we cannot compensate you a penny. That
is wrong. I am asking this Committee to step and hold EPA's feet
to the fire.

Thank you.

Senator UDALL. Thank you very much. I could not agree with you
more.

I have one final question for Governor Chavarria. Santa Clara
has had five presidential disaster declarations. Three have been as
a sub-grantee pursuant to requests made by the State of New Mexico and two issued directly to the Pueblo by the President.

How would you compare the two approaches? Can you explain to the Committee the advantages and disadvantages of each approach? Would you prefer to use one or the other in the future?

Mr. CHAVARRIA. Let me start from the last and go back. I do not want to experience another disaster. It is a headache, it is time consuming but because of build up in terms of capacity and capabilities, we have shown that our tribe is capable of implementing and utilizing these Federal dollars to our best advantage.

We even had the Office of OIG come out and do audits of the use of those funds. Those audits came back clean.

For me, it is up to us as tribal leaders, the tribal council, as a direct grantee to have the opportunity to tell your own story. Identify your specific needs. Again, having that tribal mitigation plan is crucial.

If you go with a sub-grantee, you are letting someone else tell the story for you, having the State tell the story and identify your needs, your infrastructure damage. Then you have to use their State mitigation plan. You absorb 25 percent of the cost if you go as a direct grantee. If you go as a sub-grantee, you are indebted for 12.5 percent of that cost.

The most important thing is the technical support from the Federal agency which is FEMA. Another thing as a con, if you go as a sub-grantee, you do not get the 324 administrative costs. All the tribes still have administrative burdens, so we are not guaranteed those administrative costs.

However, as the direct grantee, you are guaranteed 3.37 percent of the total cost to come down and help with administrative burdens. That is very important. We see that smaller projects receive quick funding responses from FEMA while the larger projects such as a permanent road and water control facilities remain mired in time consuming, quality assurance, quality control processes.

While clearly important, these processes greatly lengthen the review time. Time is of the essence in preventing or mitigating a natural disaster. For Santa Clara Pueblo as we enter the monsoon season, we spend our days scanning the skies and read the weather reports, fearing the worst and praying for the best.

Receiving funds that support recovery efforts prior to seasonal impacts and monsoons is imperative in breaking the cycle of continued damage. As our presidential disaster declaration experience demonstrates, in emergencies, project implementation is crucial to protecting lives, securing our communities and preventing repeated damage to key infrastructure of Santa Clara.

As I mentioned, we are not wealthy financially. I have been asked to combine all five disaster declarations but I was told, no, because each disaster is its own disaster. I cannot combine all five when then helps me financially.

Right now we are going through all disaster project worksheets and determining are these still feasible? If not, let us take that one back and give it to the Federal Government because ultimately it comes back to the cost match.

Those are the things our staff is reviewing and determining but ultimately closing out these projects is essential because that is where reimbursement comes into play.

Senator UDALL. Thank you very much. Thanks to all of the witnesses.

Thank you for your courtesies, Mr. Chairman. I appreciate it. I am sorry to run over.

The CHAIRMAN. Absolutely. No problem at all.

If there are no more questions for today, members may also submit written follow-up questions for the record. The hearing record will be open for two weeks.

With that, I would also like to express my thanks to you, Vice Chairman, and to all of our witnesses. Thank you for being here. We appreciate it very much.

With that, this hearing is concluded.

[Whereupon, at 4:33 p.m., the Committee was adjourned.]

APPENDIX

PREPARED STATEMENT OF JEFF HANSEN, DIRECTOR, OFFICE OF EMERGENCY MANAGEMENT, CHOCTAW NATION OF OKLAHOMA

Good afternoon. Mr. Chairman, members of the Committee, my name is Jeff Hansen and I am the Director of the Office of Emergency Management for the Choctaw Nation of Oklahoma. On behalf of our Chief, the Honorable Gary Batton, I thank you for this opportunity to provide testimony on FEMA's role in Indian Country.

It is my responsibility to ensure that the Choctaw Nation of Oklahoma develops and maintains a robust Emergency Management Program for our tribal service area, for our tribal citizens, and for our neighbors. I have had oversight of the emergency management program for the past four years and have worked diligently to develop the capabilities necessary to respond to any potential disaster that may arise. Our capabilities have grown from a piece-meal response initiative to a coordinated effort through many departments within the Nation. We have reached many milestones in this time, but there is still more to do.

The Choctaw Nation jurisdictional boundaries cover a 10 ½ county-wide area in southeastern Oklahoma encompassing approximately 1 1,000 square miles. This mostly rural area has a Census 2010 population of 233,126. Of that, approximately 42,000 are Choctaw tribal members. The Choctaw Nation shares governmental responsibilities for our citizens and our neighbors with state and various local units of government. Because our Indian Country lands were divided and distributed, in the form of fee-simple properties, to Choctaw Nation citizens in the late 1800s and early 1900s, we face a somewhat different approach to emergencies than do Indian tribes who have been able to maintain a contiguous reservation land base. Our tribal government responsibilities are necessarily intertwined with the governmental responsibilities of our neighboring towns, cities, counties and states.

Not unlike the rest of Oklahoma, the Choctaw Nation has experienced and responded to numerous disasters. Annually, we face the potential for any number of emergencies, including ice storms, tornadoes, floods, hazardous materials releases, high winds, drought, wildfires, transportation incidents, to name a few. In every instance, the Choctaw Nation of Oklahoma responds with both personnel and resources to address not only the needs of our people but also the non-tribal citizens within our jurisdiction. We have also responded to areas outside the Choctaw Nation to assist our fellow Oklahomans. It is our belief that we must all work closely in partnership with one another to provide the most good for the most people possible in times of disaster need.

The Choctaw Nation of Oklahoma applauds the work of this Committee, Mr. Chairman, and of the entire Congress on its effort to improve the Stafford Act through the Sandy Recovery Improvement Act. The ability for tribes to request a disaster declaration through the President of the United States is a remarkable step forward in the recognition of the Nation-to-Nation relationship and Trust Responsibility of the Federal Government and Indian Country. I believe the relationship between Tribes and specifically the Federal Emergency Management Agency have improved exponentially in recent years. However, there is still more work to be completed.

With last month's release of the Tribal Declarations Pilot Guidance, we can see the culmination of several years of work toward active consultation with tribes throughout the country. FEMA held over 100 meetings around the country from 2014 to 2016. I personally participated in at least 10 listening and consultation sessions through various settings. In every session, I heard Indian Country make our voices heard in regards to emergency management. According to FEMA, it received and adjudicated almost 2000 comments in regards to the Pilot Guidance during that time. As we progress through the pilot stage of this Pilot Guidance, there will be opportunity to review some of the issues that arise. However, FEMA should address some issues during the pilot phase of the Pilot Guidance.

The Pilot Guidance allows the chief executive of a tribe to decide what direction the tribe would like to pursue in regards to a declaration. Specifically, the chief executive can either request a declaration directly to the federal government or re-quest a declaration as a sub-grantee or recipient to the state. One of the most press-ing issues with the ability for a tribe to decide whether to go directly to the federal government or through a state is the political landscape in which it functions. In the case of Indian tribes in Oklahoma, and many other "checkerboard" tribal na-tions, this issue can be tricky to navigate. Because we do not have contiguous lands, damages to our infrastructure can be very widespread. If the Choctaw Nation elects to go directly to the federal government for a declaration, our damages are removed from state calculations. This could lead to a situation where a particular county has reportable damages but fails to meet its individual county threshold without our damages included. While the tribe may receive a declaration, the county in which the damages occurred may not qualify for assistance. This could potentially leave a particular jurisdiction with a large amount of disaster related costs that it cannot afford. As a good neighbor, an Indian tribe must decide what is best for the whole community. Unfortunately, the county cannot go to the tribe as a sub-grantee in the same manner that the tribe can go to the state. That should be fixed with authority written into federal law.

A second potential issue is with a tribe's ability to handle the personnel and regu-latory burden following a disaster. While this will depend upon a tribe's capability, it is still relatively unknown what the current capability levels are within Indian Country emergency management. Many individuals have expressed the need for emergency management programs to grow within Indian Country; hard data sup-porting that need remains as anecdotal evidence. For many years, states have re-ceived funding through the Emergency Management Performance Grant program. Unfortunately, the manner in which the law was written prohibits Indian Country from directly participating in the program. States and territories use EMPG funds use in a variety of ways to support the implementation of the National Prepared-ness System by supporting the building, sustainment, and delivery of the core capa-bilities as defined within the National Preparedness Goal. The states and territories receive funds from this program based on a population-share basis. Each state de-termines how the money is spent. In most cases, tribes can apply to the state for funding. However, this is not always the case. Grant programs supporting the devel-opment of the core capabilities with tribal set-asides remain limited. The statute should be improved with more tribal set-asides.

Lastly, FEMA has worked to expand its outreach to tribes through the appoint-ment of full time Tribal Liaisons. While this effort has definitely improved relation-ships, a few FEMA regions remain limited in outreach capability due to large num-ber of tribes and limited FEMA personnel. Within FEMA Regions 6, 9, and 10 there are a total of 478 tribes. Currently, Regions 6 and 9 have only one Tribal Liaison each while Region 10 has four Tribal Liaisons. The amount of travel required to en-gage this many tribes is daunting. Limited staffing at the FEMA regional offices that deal directly with tribes creates a roadblock in the tribes being able to develop their programs and have meaningful relationships with FEMA.

We do not have all the answers but I would like to make some suggestions that will may help to move Tribal Emergency Management Programs and their relation-ship with FEMA forward. We would ask that this Committee persuade FEMA to look into the potential to have local jurisdictions request assistance as sub-grantee recipients to the tribes in the event they do not meet their threshold when a tribe receives a disaster declaration. This step would provide a more unified approach be-tween the states and tribes as we assist our common communities in common dis-aster contexts.

We would also ask that this Committee work within Congress to address funding opportunities for tribes within the emergency management field. The lack of avail-able funding continues to be a major issue in the establishment and enhancement of emergency management core capabilities in Indian Country. Targeting to Indian tribes funds like those released in the EMPG program would allow tribes to begin building capacity and becoming an asset to local and state jurisdictions during a cri-sis.

Lastly, we ask that this Committee urge FEMA to expand its Tribal Liaison pro-gram to assist in those regions where the majority of tribes reside. Additionally, funding for training opportunities through FEMA will assist in preparing tribal emergency management staff for the tasks associated with the declaration process and the regulatory paperwork to follow a disaster.

Again, thank you for the opportunity to provide testimony to the Committee. It is an honor to be able to provide updates and background to the situations we face in Indian Country. The Choctaw Nation of Oklahoma is committed to better pre-paring our communities for disasters and working with our partner agencies to respond and recover. Your continued support is critical to the reduction of disaster impacts across all of Indian Country. Yakoke!

————

RESPONSE TO WRITTEN QUESTIONS SUBMITTED BY HON. TOM UDALL TO ALEX AMPARO

Question 1. What types of coordination efforts have there been to update Tribal on the process and requirements for requesting Stafford Act declarations?

Answer. In coordination with FEMA's National Tribal Affairs Advisor and FEMA Regional Tribal Liaisons, FEMA Recovery Directorate and Office of External Affairs Tribal Partners Branch hosted two national webinars/conference calls on the final version of the Tribal Declarations Pilot Guidance, which included information on the process and requirements for requesting Stafford Act declarations.

In addition, FEMA continues to provide briefings at national and Regional Tribal conferences and for individual Tribes when requested.

Question 2. What actions has FEMA taken to help Tribes understand what Federal resources are available to build and maintain their emergency management capacity?

Answer. FEMA is committed to partnering and collaborating with Federally recognized Indian Tribes, and to providing resources to support their preparation for, protection against, mitigation of, response to, and recovery from all hazards and disasters.

FEMA established both a Tribal Policy and Tribal Consultation Policy that provide the framework for FEMA Tribal relations, and guides how the agency delivers technical assistance and programs tailored to the unique circumstances of Tribal communities.

FEMA offers various resources to support Tribes. This includes:

- Information Sharing and Program Support: sharing information with, and receiving feedback from Tribes on issues and resources that impact their communities;

- Technical Assistance and Grant Opportunities: assisting Tribes with technical assistance and providing awareness of available grants that assist in building Tribal emergency management capability and capacity;

- Training and Exercises: providing access to training at FEMA facilities and local Tribal venues to strengthen Tribes ability to respond to emergencies by addressing identified gaps and weaknesses; and

- Tribal Consultation: working with Tribes to collect their feedback on potential FEMA Tribal policies and actions to ensure we are in compliance with EO 13175.

These areas, described in more detail below, ensure a consistent interaction with our Tribal partners and offers Tribes a platform to work with FEMA.

Information Sharing and Program Support

FEMA's National Tribal Affairs Advisor (NTAA), in the Headquarters (HQ) Office of External Affairs, Tribal Partners Branch (TPB), is the senior advisor on Tribal issues to the FEMA Administrator and senior leadership. FEMA Regional Tribal Liaisons (RTLs) serve as the main points of contact for Tribal nations, and are directly contacted by Tribes for technical assistance or questions about available Federal resources. The NTAA engages regularly with the national Tribal associations to discuss policy issues with national implications for Tribes while RTLs regularly provide information to Tribal nations on FEMA programs, resources, and grant opportunities. They help coordinate technical assistance through various mechanisms—direct contact via meetings and calls with Tribal emergency managers on a regular basis, conference calls or webinars with Tribes in their regions or Regional Tribal associations, attending and presenting at Tribal conferences, and visiting and briefing Tribes in person.

The HQ TPB hosts a monthly conference call with Tribal associations and organizations to discuss and share information to support emergency management efforts in Indian Country. In addition, FEMA's Office of External Affairs includes Tribal partners when FEMA sends out advisories to notify when a grant application period begins or when there are other opportunities to engage or participate. FEMA's Office of External Affairs also developed a "FEMA and Tribal Nations" pocket guide, which provides information and resources that may be helpful to Tribal partners. Distributed at Tribal conferences and meetings, the pocket guide explains the Agency's policies related to Tribal engagement, outlines key FEMA programs and how they specifically relate to Tribes, and provides contact information for the Agency's Tribal liaisons. This active engagement and frequent contact allows our Tribal partners to have visibility on FEMA programs and services as they change and evolve.

Technical Assistance and Grant Opportunities

FEMA continues to improve its education, outreach, and technical assistance to Tribes to help them become more aware of available Federal resources such as technical assistance and eligible Federal grants. For example, FEMA provides technical assistance to Tribes on the Threat and Hazard Identification and Risk Assessment (THIRA), a process for jurisdictions to identify their greatest threats and hazards and ways to address them. Having a complete THIRA is a requirement for Tribal applicants applying for a Tribal Homeland Security Grant, which provides funding directly to eligible Tribes to strengthen their capacity to prepare for and respond to emergencies.

The Federal Insurance and Mitigation Administration (FIMA) supports Tribal governments by providing guidance, training, and technical assistance in the development and/or update of FEMA approved Hazard Mitigation Plans and in the development of Hazard Mitigation Assistance (HMA) planning and project grants. Hazard mitigation planning enables Tribal governments to identify risks and vulnerabilities associated with natural disasters, and develop long-term strategies for protecting people and property from future hazard events.

Training and Exercises

FEMA's Emergency Management Institute (EMI) provides training to Tribal governments and their employees to develop their emergency management capabilities. FEMA through EMI, engages with Tribes to design courses that reflect Tribal needs and gaps in capabilities. EMI provides housing during the training and reimburses participants for their travel costs. In addition to providing Tribal curriculum courses at FEMA facilities, EMI also provides these courses off-site, traveling out to Tribal communities directly. To date, more than 3,000 certificates of completion have been issued for courses in the EMI Tribal Curriculum. EMI currently has planned 21 courses on their 2017 schedule. Additionally, EMI provides Tribal emergency management officials access to 550 courses.

FEMA's Center for Domestic Preparedness (CDP) also provides training to Tribal emergency responders. In fiscal year 2016, CDP hosted its first Tribal Nations Training Week and trained 157 Tribal emergency responders from 46 Tribal nations. More than 150 Tribal emergency responders from 41 Tribal agencies across the country, trained at CDP during their second Tribal Nations Training Week from March 19–25, 2017. CDP worked closely with Tribal students to enhance their capability to respond to disasters and emergencies by taking one or more of the seven courses delivered during the week.

In addition to providing training, FEMA also coordinates exercises with Tribal nations to examine and validate readiness capabilities. In September 2015, FEMA Region VIII and HQ TPB worked with seven Tribal nations to coordinate a simulated exercise as part of Operation Safe Delivery in response to a crude oil train derailment on the Blackfeet Nation Reservation. In June 2016, FEMA Region X conducted a four-day functional earthquake and tsunami exercise, Cascadia Rising, and worked with 24 Tribes in Washington, Oregon, and Idaho. During these exercises, FEMA examined its internal capacity to understand and respond to the unique needs of Tribal governments. FEMA also invites Tribal governments in hurricane-prone areas to participate in FEMA's annual hurricane preparedness video teleconference with FEMA leadership and State emergency management directors.

Tribal Consultation

FEMA's Tribal Consultation Policy establishes how the agency engages Tribes in meaningful consultation to influence FEMA policies, programs, and the resources supporting these efforts. The NTAA and HQ TPB work closely with all FEMA programmatic offices and Regions to ensure that FEMA policies take into consideration the unique needs and capabilities of Tribes, and engages these offices to plan their Tribal consultation outreach. This consultation outreach effort is worked through the RTLs allowing an agency wide effort to give Tribes the opportunity to be involved in the developing process of FEMA's policies, programs, and resources. The Consultation Policy provides an opportunity for Tribal governments to request Tribal consultation on a policy or action by FEMA that they determine affects their community or has Tribal implications. Tribal consultation is announced through in-person events, Tribal meetings, monthly conference calls with Tribes and other agencies, and through Intergovernmental Affairs advisories.

Tribal nations are a critical part of FEMA's whole community effort to improve emergency management capabilities and capacity across the nation and we remain committed to working with Tribes on a nation-to-nation basis.

Question 3. The disaster declaration process was developed for State governments, which generally have a larger tax base, receive more grant funds, and have decades of experience managing Federally declared major disasters. In comparison to the States, do Tribes have a similar level of Federal resources available to them to help manage the post-declaration recovery process?

Answer. The Sandy Recovery Improvement Act (SRIA) of 2013 (SRIA) amended the Stafford Act to provide Federally-recognized Indian Tribal governments the option to make a direct request to the President for a major disaster or emergency declaration or to seek assistance under a state's state declaration. Prior to SRIA State governments had primary access to Federal resources to help them manage the post-declaration recovery process, as compared to Indian Tribal governments. Today, due to SRIA, Tribes have direct access to FEMA response and recovery programs. In addition, our understanding is that there are other Federal government agencies that provide recovery resources to States and Tribes.

Question 4. What assistance has FEMA offered, or could FEMA offer, to help enhance Tribal capacity to manage the recovery process?

Answer. Technical assistance, through FEMA Regional Tribal Liaisons (located in all FEMA Regional offices), is one way that FEMA is working to overcome potential access issues. Before, during, and after disaster FEMA provides technical assistance and trainings to Indian Tribal governments on various administrative requirements for Stafford Act disaster assistance, including Preliminary Damage Assessments, administrative plans, mitigation plans, and grants management requirements. FEMA also provides field leadership to support Indian Tribal governments in addressing, organizing and managing disaster response and recovery activities through Federal Coordinating Officers and Federal Disaster Recovery Coordinators.

Question 5. FEMA can authorize its crisis counseling program as part of an individual assistance package. Some IHS facilities also offer mental health services to Native Americans. How does access to mental health services at IHS affect FEMA's recommendation to provide crisis counseling services in Tribal communities?

Answer. States, territories and federally recognized Tribes can apply for grant funding for the FEMA Crisis Counseling Assistance and Training Program (CCP) in the wake of presidentially declared major disasters which have received a designation for Individual Assistance. As a supplemental program, CCP services are meant to supplement and not supplant or replace existing behavioral health (mental health and substance abuse) services. As part of the application, the grantee is asked to describe State/Tribal and local mental health services and explain why they cannot meet the disaster-related mental health needs caused or aggravated by the disaster. Once FEMA determines that the disaster overwhelmed the existing behavioral health capacity (including IHS capacity), the State/territory/Tribe may receive CCP grant funding.

Question 6. Since the enactment of the Tribal Stafford Act, tribes have made twenty requests and the President has declared eight disasters in response.

Describe each request and the basis for FEMA's recommendation to approve or deny those requests.

Answer. The President has sole discretion to approve emergency and major disaster declarations. For every request, in making a recommendation to the President, FEMA considers the Joint Preliminary Damage Assessment provided by the Tribe, whether the Tribal resources have been overwhelmed, and the extent to which Stafford Act programs can address the needs created by the event and provide supplemental assistance.

Question 7. In its 2014 testimony, FEMA stated that it received eight direct Tribal requests and declared six major disasters. That is a seventy-five percent success rate. As of January 31, 2017, FEMA received twenty Tribal requests, and the President declared eight major disasters. That brings the overall success rate to forty percent since the enactment of the Tribal Stafford Act.

Please explain the markedly lower rate of declared disasters since FEMA testified in 2014.

Are states denied disaster assistance at the same or a similar rate as Tribes? Please explain and address any reasons for the disparity.

Answer. Many Indian Tribal governments (Tribal governments) are less experienced than states with the disaster declaration process and Stafford Act programs. This has resulted in some Tribes seeking assistance for events that are either not eligible or cannot be readily addressed by Stafford Act programs (i.e. impacts to fishing, impacts of drought, erosion, etc.). There was a 47 percent approval rate for

Tribal declarations and 83 percent for state declarations (some of which included Tribal entities as recipients or sub recipients) during the period of January 29, 2013 and January 31, 2017. We are continuing our outreach and education efforts to ensure that all Tribal governments have a comprehensive understanding of Stafford Act declarations.

In addition, requests received prior to publication of the Tribal Declarations Pilot Guidance, were processed using the guidance for state declaration requests, including a $1 million threshold for Public Assistance and a per capita indicator. After three rounds of consultation with Tribes, FEMA published the Tribal Declarations Pilot Guidance, which provides unique factors, including a new minimum damage amount of $250,000, for FEMA to consider that better take into account the unique circumstances of Tribal governments.

Question 8. FEMA noted in its 2014 testimony that the regulations may be ill-suited to tribal requests because the regulations were designed for states.

How does the Pilot Guidance account for the unique status of tribes?

Does FEMA consider the federal trust responsibility when recommending a decision to the President? If so, how?

Answer. FEMA acknowledges the trust responsibility of the federal government to federally recognized Tribal governments as established by specific treaties, court decisions, statutes, executive orders, regulations, and policies. Specifically, in recognition of this trust responsibility and as prescribed by Congress in the Sandy Recovery Improvement Act, FEMA is implementing the Tribal Declarations Pilot Guidance (the Guidance) for direct emergency and disaster declarations.

The Tribal Declarations Pilot Guidance provides new, specially designed, criteria for evaluating an Indian Tribal government's request for a disaster declaration, and takes into account the unique conditions that affect Tribal nations. This criteria was developed as a result of extensive consultation and listening sessions with Tribes. For example, the Public Assistance minimum damage amount of $250,000 for Tribal declarations (versus $1 million minimum for states). Absent extraordinary circumstances, when preliminary damage assessments indicate $250,000 in PA-eligible damage and costs, FEMA will then look holistically at the impacts to and capabilities of a Tribal nation to determine the need for supplemental federal assistance.

In addition, the guidance provides for eligibility under the Individuals and Households Program for enrolled Tribal members, and at the request of the Tribal nation, members of the Tribal community who are not enrolled Tribal members.

Question 9. FEMA testified in 2014 that it developed the Emergency Management Institute Tribal curriculum to help Tribes with their emergency response activities.

Has the curriculum evolved since then, if so, how?

Answer. Yes the curriculum continues evolving by including emerging policies, highlighting best practices and discussing case studies. Recently, FEMA's Office of Response and Recovery delivered a presentation discussing the Tribal Declarations Guidance and provided an informational briefing, fact sheet, and frequently asked questions to each student. During the consultation period, FEMA staff utilized the course presentations as an opportunity to conduct consultation on the Declaration Guidance.

Question 10. Has FEMA updated the curriculum to include the Pilot Guidance?

Answer. Yes. Immediately after passage of the Sandy Recovery Improvement Act of 2013, the Tribal Curriculum course deliveries included a presentation segment for the Tribal Declaration Guidance. The presentation explained FEMA's implementa- tion plan for the authority. In addition, the students received the presentation, fact sheets, and frequently asked questions. Additionally, these documents were used outside of the course delivery materials for consultation during the development of implementation guidance.

Since the Pilot Period commenced on January 10, 2017, the Emergency Management Institute initiated the development of appropriate training material to be incorporated into the Tribal Curriculum courses, and is currently assisting in the development of other complementary training material to be delivered by FEMA Regional Offices. In addition, Emergency Management Institute is developing Tribal Declaration reusable learning object content to be made open source available to the whole community for inclusion in other training.

The Center for Domestic Preparedness (CDP) has a lasting commitment to Tribal Nations training. As part of an ongoing outreach effort, CDP hosted 157 Tribal students from 41 Tribes enrolled in five different training programs during the CDP 2017 Tribal Nations Training Week, March 20–24, 2017. This is the second annual Tribal Nations Training Week which has proven to be a highly successful outreach tool focused on specific Tribal training needs. CDP invited members of the National Domestic Preparedness Consortium, Rural Domestic Preparedness Consortium, and the Emergency Management Institute to make short presentations during the week. The week culminated with a fully operational mass casualty exercise featuring a multi-disciplinary response to a simulated disaster.

Thus far in FY17, CDP has trained 266 Tribal Nations students for a total of 483 course completions which is 5.8 percent of the resident training population.

Question 11. Preparing a disaster declaration request is resource-intensive, and resources often get stretched thin during emergency response.

What type of technical assistance does FEMA provide to Tribes while preparing their declaration requests?

Does FEMA provide sample documents that would give Tribal officials an idea of what an ideal request would look like?

Answer. Before, during, and after disaster FEMA provides technical assistance and trainings to Indian Tribal governments (Tribal governments) on various administrative requirements for Stafford Act disaster assistance, including Preliminary Damage Assessments, administrative plans, mitigation plans, and grants management.

On March 21, 2017, a Cover Letter Template for Tribal governments was posted to www.fema.gov to assist Tribal governments in submitting declaration requests which meet the criteria outlined in the Tribal Declarations Pilot Guidance.

Each FEMA region has a Regional Tribal Liaison that works with the Tribes on requests for technical assistance, and can provide Regional resources prior to disasters to answer questions and guide them through the disaster declaration process. Both the region and HQ Tribal staff have facilitated many meetings with Tribal officials to discuss areas of concern and questions they may have on disaster programs and resources.

Question 12. The Pilot Guidance stresses the importance of having emergency plans, mitigation plans, and administrative plans prepared in advance of disaster events.

Please explain how tribes may successfully develop each plan and describe any best practices for developing each type of plan.

Tribes have described preparation of these plans as both time and resource intensive. Please provide specifics on how FEMA provides technical assistance to assist tribes in preparing each type of plan.

Answer. At the request of Indian Tribal governments (Tribal governments), training and technical assistance can be provided in a variety of ways, including training in-person (field delivered or in-residence at FEMA's Emergency Management Institute), or remote, and online, for developing a Tribal Mitigation Plan, Public Assistance Administrative Plan, Hazard Mitigation Administrative Plan, Tribal Administrative Plan and how to complete the Other Needs Assistance Option Selection form. FEMA encourages Tribal officials to contact their Regional Tribal Liaison or FEMA Regional Recovery and Mitigation Planning staff to request technical assistance, if needed. We are also working with Tribes to develop other resources that can assist them in meeting the planning requirements, such as the Tribal Mitigation Planning Guidance (described below) which is now in consultation.

Other Needs Assistance Administrative Option Selection form and Tribal Administrative Plan

Prior to assistance being provided, FEMA must have a current, approved Other Needs Assistance (ONA) Administrative Option Selection form and Tribal Administrative Plan (TAP), if applicable, on file. The ONA Administrative Option Selection form is a standard FEMA form where the Tribal government elects which entity will administer ONA (FEMA, Tribe, or a joint effort) and establishes assistance limits for specific ONA items and maximum award amounts for transportation, funeral, and child care assistance. In situations where the Tribal government elects to administer ONA jointly with FEMA or by itself, the Tribal government must also submit an Administrative Plan, which outlines the procedures that the Tribal government will use to administer assistance. FEMA can assist in this decisionmaking and provide technical assistance in the development of these plans.

FEMA Regional staff are the best point of contact for Tribal leaders when filling out their ONA forms or in developing a TAP. Many regions are currently conducting outreach to Tribal governments to assist them in navigating the ONA process.

Tribal Mitigation Plan

It is important that Tribes begin the process of developing or updating a mitigation plan, as far in advance as possible as the process can require longer than a year and possibly more than two years if the Tribal government seeks to fund the plan with a grant. Information on potentially available planning grants can be found on FEMA's Hazard Mitigation Assistance website.

The steps involved in developing a mitigation plan include:

1. Organization of resources—this includes the formation of the planning team and other partnerships and technical resources needed to move through the key planning steps. Some Tribes may have the capability and capacity to do this on their own. Others may choose to work with a consultant. Regardless, a strong Tribal planning team and process is the key to a successful mitigation program.

2. Assessment of risk—identification of the potential hazards that could affect the Tribal area, and the people, property and other assets, that are potentially vulnerable to these hazards.

3. Development of a mitigation strategy—the mitigation strategy is the heart of the plan. Based on the findings of the risk assessment, the Tribal government develops a course of action, including goals and actions to address the risks. This includes the prioritization of potential actions based on the Tribal government's capabilities, (existing plans, programs, personnel, funding and other factors).

4. Implementation, plan monitoring and plan updates: The Tribal government can bring the mitigation plan to life in a variety of ways, from implementing specific mitigation projects to integrating the mitigation actions into existing Tribal government programs and initiatives. It is important for the plan to remain current and relevant with respect to risk and Tribal capabilities. Periodic evaluations to assess changing risks and priorities will enable the Tribal government to ensure the plan continues to meet the Tribe's needs, and help the Tribe prepare for a potential disaster.

Tribal governments can find mitigation planning resources online, including the Tribal Hazard Mitigation Planning Guidance, which includes some best practices. Regions can assist Tribes by connecting them with examples and some best practices and examples of Tribal mitigation plans can be found in the Homeland Security Digital Library, by using search terms "Tribal mitigation plan."

Hazard Mitigation Administrative Plans

The Hazard Mitigation Administrative Plan is a procedural guide that details how the Tribal government will administer the HMGP. The Tribal government must have a current administrative plan approved by the appropriate FEMA Regional Administrator before receiving HMGP funds. The administrative plan may take any form including a chapter within a comprehensive Tribal mitigation program strategy. The Tribal government may forward an administrative plan to FEMA for approval at any time prior to or immediately after the request for a disaster declaration. An approved plan is a prerequisite of receiving HMGP funds and is used by FEMA in determining approval for and the amount of each grant.

The Administrative Plan, must establish procedures to guide the following 13 activities, and FEMA will review the information provided to ensure proper documentation of each activity:

1.Identify and notify potential sub applicants of the availability of HMGP funding.

2.Provide, as applicable, potential sub applicants with information on the application process, program eligibility, and deadlines.

3.Determine sub applicant eligibility, as applicable.

4.Provide information for EHP and floodplain management reviews.

5.Process requests for advances of funds and reimbursements.

6.Monitor and evaluate the progress and completion of funded mitigation activities.

7.Review and approve cost overruns.

8.Process appeals.

9.Provide technical assistance as required to sub recipients, as applicable.

10.Comply with the administrative requirements of 44 CFR Part 206 and 2 CFR Part 200.

11.Comply with audit requirements of 2 CFR Part 200 Subpart F.

12.Provide quarterly progress reports to FEMA on funded mitigation activities.

FEMA Mitigation regularly holds mitigation training courses at the Emergency Management Institute and disaster operation offices (JFO); provides updates and general information to national audiences at various stakeholder engagement meetings (e.g., National Emergency Management Association, HMA Workshop); and hosts Regional meetings between FEMA Regions and Regional partners. Additionally, FEMA has written guidance in the Hazard Mitigation Assistance Guidance (published February 27, 2015) on the requirement and development of an administrative plan.

Emergency Plans

FEMA's Tribal Curriculum course *Emergency Management Framework for Tribal Governments* does provide training in the development of emergency plans. Since the development of the course in 2012, FEMA has provided examples of Tribal Emergency Plans to course participants.

Question 13. Please describe how the National Disaster Recovery Framework functions, including which agencies participate in the Framework, and the resources it may provide to a Tribe that requests Federal disaster recovery assistance.

Are Tribes and States eligible for the same number and types of assistance under the Framework? Please list and describe any assistance that is unavailable to Tribes and any assistance only available to Tribes as sub-recipients of a State.

Answer. The National Disaster Recovery Framework (NDRF) provides the architecture for organizing agencies to better leverage existing Federal programs and support, de-conflict Federally support activities, and maximize the impact of Federal funds and nongovernmental resources to meet Tribal and survivor needs. The Framework does not provide additional funding or resources beyond existing Federal authorities.

In coordination with the Federal Coordinating Officer (FCO), the State or Tribal Coordinating Officer, and the community impacted, the Federal Disaster Recovery Coordinator (FDRC) will determine which additional Federal agencies are needed to support the recovery mission. The FDRC helps to serve as a single representative to facilitate identification of needs and provision of recovery resources from a variety of resources. In collaboration with the FDRC, six Federal departments and agencies coordinate Recovery Support Functions for core sectors: Economic; Health and Social Services; Housing; Infrastructure Systems; Natural and Cultural Resources; and Community Planning and Capacity Building. Additional information about the Recovery Support Functions, including lists of the participating agencies are available on FEMA's website: *https://www.fema.gov/recovery-support-functions.*

The FDRC will convene Federal recovery interagency and nongovernmental partners as a coordinating body in support of the impacted community, Tribe, or State's recovery goals. Depending on the disaster requirements, agency representatives will deploy directly to the Joint Field Office and the area of impact to provide technical assistance to the Federal operation, assess the impacts, and develop a joint strategy for supporting the Tribe's and/or State's recovery goals. As part of the strategic solutions process, agencies identify programs under their own authorities that may be appropriate to assist the recovery goals of the impacted community.

Note that some Federal program authorities are exclusive to Tribal governments, and some programs are only accessible through a State government. For instance, US Department of Housing and Urban Development, Environmental Protection Agency, Indian Health Service, and US Department of Transportation all have Tribal-specific programs for which a State would not qualify. Similarly, some non-disaster State pass-through programs, such as US Department of Health and Human Services Low Income Home Energy Assistance Program, may be accessible if the Tribe applies to the State. Some agency authorities distinguish between States and Tribes, others do not.

Question 14. Please describe how the Recovery Support Strategy relates to the Framework and how Tribal views are meaningfully considered during the Strategy's development.

Answer. Under the National Disaster Recovery Framework, the Federal Disaster Recovery Coordinator and activated Recovery Support Functions develop a Recovery Support Strategy (RSS) after a disaster to organize Federal support and resources to assist with local recovery priorities and goals. The FDRC and partner agencies engage local leaders and stakeholders to better understand Tribal, community, and State recovery goals. In essence, the RSS is a road map that determines how existing and available Federal resources will be used to support local recovery needs and priorities.

For the Community of Galena, Alaska (which has both a city council and a Tribal council [Louden Alaska Native Village]), residents were invited to participate in two structured goal-setting sessions. Representatives from Federal and State agencies met directly with the community members to talk through issues, feasibility, funding options, and lessons learned from other communities, in order to help with the identification of possible projects. The representatives from Galena identified about 200 possible projects, then selected about 30 priority projects. These projects became the basis of the RSS (copy available upon request). Participating Federal agencies included US Army Corps of Engineers; National Renewable Energy Lab (US Department of Energy); Economic Development Administration (US Department of Commerce); FEMA; and US Department of Housing and Urban Development. State and Federal agencies collectively agreed to honor the project descriptions as written and not modify them without agreement from the community.

For the Oglala Sioux Tribe (OST), the OST President identified the over-arching priorities of "Health, Housing, and Roads" for the Federal recovery strategic focus. The OST President designated the Tribal Coordinating Officer to work directly with the Federal partners, and designated specific Tribal department directors to work with the Federal agencies. The RSS for OST (copy available upon request) evolved from direct interaction between the Tribal leadership and Tribal department heads and the Federal agency representatives. Participating Federal agencies included US Department of Housing and Urban Development; US Department of Agriculture-Rural Development; US Army Corps of Engineers; US Department of Energy—National Renewable Energy Lab; and US Department of Transportation—Federal Highways Administration.

———

RESPONSE TO WRITTEN QUESTIONS SUBMITTED BY HON. HEIDI HEITKAMP TO ALEX AMPARO

Question 1. What is FEMA's plan for continuing dialogue with Indian Tribes during the Tribal declaration pilot program?

Answer. In coordination with FEMA's National Tribal Affairs Advisor and FEMA Regional Tribal Liaisons, FEMA Recovery Directorate and Office of External Affairs Tribal Partners Branch hosted two national webinars/conference calls on the final version of the Tribal Declarations Pilot Guidance, which included information on the process and requirements for requesting Stafford Act declarations.

In addition, FEMA continues to work with Regional Tribal Liaisons on nationwide Tribal engagement surrounding declarations and the Guidance and to provide briefings at national and Regional Tribal conferences and for individual Tribes, when desired.

Question 2. How is the formula for tribal declarations different from state declarations?

What methods did FEMA use to determine the formula?

Answer. The Tribal Declarations Pilot Guidance provides new, specially designed, criteria for evaluating a Tribal government's request for a disaster declaration and takes into account the unique conditions which affect Tribal nations. This criteria was developed as a result of extensive consultation and listening sessions with Tribes.

For example, the Public Assistance (PA) minimum damage amount of $250,000 for Tribal declarations (versus $1 million dollar minimum for States). Absent extraordinary circumstances, when preliminary damage assessments indicate $250,000 in PA-eligible damage and costs, FEMA will then look holistically at the impacts to and capabilities of a Tribal nation to determine the need for supplemental Federal assistance.

Immediately following the first round of consultation for the guidance, FEMA proposed a figure of $1 million dollar requirement for PA for Tribes with populations greater than 10,000 members. For Tribes that had less than 10,000 members, they had to meet at $500,000 dollar requirement. For the second round of consultation, $300,000 was the proposed figure. During the final round of consultation, FEMA received feedback that the $300,000 was still too high for many Tribes, so the final Tribal Declarations Pilot Guidance provides a minimum damage amount of $250,000. The $250,000 PA minimum damage amount is based on the average administrative cost to FEMA to administer a Tribal declaration.

In addition, the guidance provides for eligibility under the Individuals and Households Program for enrolled Tribal members, and at the request of the Tribal nation, members of the Tribal community who are not enrolled Tribal members.

It is also important to remember that the Guidance is only a pilot and may be adjusted following the end of the pilot period.

Question 3. Given the change in the administration, how is FEMA working to make sure that all of the past accomplishments in setting up the pilot program are continuing to be used as a foundation for new goals?

Answer. FEMA's commitment to implementing the Tribal authorities under the Sandy Recovery Improvement Act (SRIA) has resulted in a culture shift in the way we work with Tribal governments and officials, and we engage with them on policies and actions that have substantial direct effects on Tribes. Throughout our programs, we have instilled a practice of ensuring that Tribes are considered when we develop policy and that we consult when impacts are identified. These practices are in support of FEMA's established Tribal Policy and Tribal Consultation Policy that provide the framework for FEMA Tribal relations and Tribal consultation, and guides how the agency delivers technical assistance and programs tailored to the unique circumstances of Tribal communities. These two policies are revised every four years to reflect new authorities and polices. The Agency created a Tribal Integration Group (TIG) focused on internal coordination and collaboration on Tribal engagement and consultation efforts across all program areas.

In the development of the Tribal Declarations Pilot Guidance, FEMA sought input from Tribal governments during three consultation periods, and received and adjudicated hundreds of comments to develop the Pilot Guidance. The Tribal consultation methods and Tribal engagement used and learned during the development of the Tribal Declarations Pilot Guidance, serve as best practices for consultations going forward. The success of the effort solidified the consultation policy as the foundation for how to conduct Tribal consultation moving forward. The National Tribal Affairs Advisor, the Office of External Affairs' Tribal Partners Branch, the Regional Tribal Liaisons, and the TIG will continue to work closely with all FEMA programmatic offices to ensure FEMA policies take into consideration the unique needs and capabilities of Tribes, that programs are adhering to the Tribal Policy, and that the agency is fully utilizing the Tribal Consultation Policy.

————

RESPONSE TO WRITTEN QUESTIONS SUBMITTED BY HON. JAMES LANKFORD TO ALEX AMPARO

Question 1. Under current law (42 USC 5122), the owner or operator of private nonprofit facilities damaged by major disasters may receive financial assistance for the repair, restoration, reconstruction, or replacement of the facility and related expenses. Private nonprofit facilities currently are defined, in part, to include "any private nonprofit facility that provides essential services of a governmental nature to the general public;" however, houses of worship are currently excluded.

During the hearing I asked whether there are any properties or structures that are excluded from a disaster declaration, and in particular, houses of worship. You indicated that sacred lands and houses of worship, would be included as Tribal infrastructure. What if that Tribal infrastructure is used for sectarian instruction or worship? In that case, could that house of worship be a recipient of FEMA disaster aid?

Answer. Even if the house of worship or other Tribal infrastructure is used for American Indian traditional religious and cultural practices, or for any other kind of sectarian instruction or worship, the facility may still be an eligible recipient of FEMA assistance.